Learning Resources
and the
Instructional Program
in
Community Colleges

LEARNING RESOURCES

AND THE

INSTRUCTIONAL
PROGRAM

IN

COMMUNITY
COLLEGES

David R. Bender

Library Professional Publications
Hamden, Connecticut
1980

First published 1980 as a
Library Professional Publication
an imprint of The Shoe String Press, Inc.
Hamden, Connecticut 06514

Printed in the United States of America

Library of Congress Cataloging and Publication Data

Bender, David R
  Learning resources and the instructional
program in community colleges

  Bibliography: p.
  Includes index.
  1. Community colleges—United States—
Curricula. 2. Instructional systems. 3. Educa-
tion, Higher—United States—Audio-visual
aids. 4. Instructional Materials Centers. I.
Title.
LB2328.B37   378'.1543   80-14567
ISBN 0-208-01754-2
ISBN 0-208-01851-4 (pbk.)

Table of Contents

To Robert, Scott, *and* Lori
for all they are and
are to be.

Acknowledgments

My thanks to all the community college personnel who so freely and willingly gave of their time in responding to the questionnaires. My sincere appreciation goes to the seven learning resources administrators and staffs who assisted me during the case studies—Sarah K. Thomson, Iole Matteucig, Richard L. Ducote, Margaret E. C. Howland, Betty Duvall, H. Keith Harker, and Leah K. Nekritz.

I am grateful for the thoughtful comments of H. Thomas Walker, which improved this book.

Finally, thanks to my editor, Virginia Mathews, for her assistance and guidance.

List of Tables

List of Figures

Foreword

Arthur Cohen, a college professor and community college consultant on curriculum and instruction, states that:

> The community junior college today represents one of the few unique accomplishments of American education in the twentieth century—expanded educational opportunity for all citizens. . . . For many of its enrollees, it is a stepping stone to the higher learning; for most, it is the last formal, graded, public education in which they will be involved. (4:xv–xvi)

Because of this unique role in providing something for nearly everyone, the community college must develop unique curricular and instructional programs which are aimed at meeting the needs of its diverse student body. A great number of community colleges have been successful in creating a learning environment which is fulfilling student needs. Thus the community college has taken its place in America's educational system.

There are numerous external factors which are affecting the rapid growth of community colleges. Among these are: population growth, knowledge explosion, increased use of technology and automation, flexible vocational specialization, obsolescence of existing knowledge in specialized areas, and an increase in leisure time. The community college must be designed to serve all persons who reside within the college's jurisdiction. Many

11

community colleges are developing instructional programs outside the traditional, formal classroom, thus being able to meet the needs of their diverse student population. Unlike other higher educational institutions, the community college is not a prisoner of past educational expectations or values. As a result, it is freer to experiment and to explore innovative programs, new curricula, and new teaching/learning techniques.

One such program is the learning resources system, yet there exists little information on the relationship of learning resources systems to instructional programs in community college settings. The available literature is scattered in a variety of publications, proceedings, house organs, and conference notes. This fragmentation has made it difficult to understand the technique and developmental stages through which learning resources systems become an integral part of the instructional program of the community college.

This book will attempt to document that the learning resource program is one of the most important instructionally oriented services of the college community. In designing instructional programs, consideration must be given to instructional materials from which students will learn as well as to teacher interaction. C. Edward Cavert, Associate Director for Instructional Design, State University of Nebraska Project, claims that a major justification for "electronically facilitated instruction" is that it enables the instructor to make learning more manageable and efficient. The learning resources center (LRC) staff is in an excellent position to assist fellow instructors in all areas of curriculum development.

The community college provides an open environment and is receptive to instructional experimentation. These are flexible institutions where new ideas for learning, with all types of resources, can be tried. The learning resources program can only be effective if it provides support facilities, materials, and staff for the entire institution. Since each community college is unique in its instructional program, the learning resources program must reflect the institution it is designed to serve. This requires continual analysis and development as the needs and programs of the college change.

Community colleges are designed specifically to serve the various needs of the students within the college's service area. Among these are (1) transfer curriculum, (2) citizenship and general education, (3) occupational training, (4) general studies, (5) adult and continuing education, (6) remedial programs, (7) counseling and guidance, and (8) co-curricular or student-activity function. Each of these functions becomes the "immediate blueprint" to be used by faculty and administration in planning operational practices, curricula, and various services and activities. (25:32–45)

Teaching, rather than research, has always been of major importance to the community college. It is, however, frequently difficult to support this emphasis because of the increasing number of students enrolling in community colleges, the lack of classroom facilities, and the fact that few people are educated for community college teaching positions. There are almost no specifically designed training programs for teaching at the community college level.

Given the lack of research about community college learning resources programs, examination of compatible research conducted in four-year institutions, public libraries, and secondary schools is the next best thing but hardly a satisfactory substitute. Community college learning resources programs must be thoroughly studied, in order to make possible the development, design, and implementation of truly effective instructionally related programs. The learning resources program can not be examined in isolation, for its very existence is dependent upon its relationship to the college's instructional program. The lack of documentation is a major problem in developing learning resources that are planned in terms of their relationship to instructional programs within the community college.

A major goal of this book is to document the role of the learning resources program and the relationship of media innovations to instructional techniques found in community colleges.

Introduction

By the late 1970's, educators had learned anew that they must be concerned with the humanistic aspects of the society and reflect that concern through their work, because education is a person-to-person enterprise. For too long, the profession has over-labeled and jargoned to death what has been its basic and primary responsibility: delivery of information and skills which meet the developmental, learning, and recreational needs of the clients to be served. No one now expects the success or superior performance of a program without carefully considering human interaction. Efforts to mechanize the "education business" and apply industrial techniques to human behavior have not worked, and education has been forced "back to the drawing boards" with the certainty that interpersonal relationships and communications are basic to effective teaching and learning. So are flexibility, alternatives, and choice of methods and learning materials. The excellence of the learning resources program is more essential now than it has ever been, especially for community college students, who must maintain a high level of motivation and interest to manage their learning, often despite conflicts caused by jobs, commuting, and a difficult home study climate.

The learning resources of the community college are influential in the development of the instructional program and must be integrated into the curricular mainstream if the college is to achieve its goals. The North Central Association of Colleges and Secondary Schools has maintained, as part of its accreditation procedures, that the learning resources program is to be conceived and developed as an integral part of the educational program of the college. The result must reflect the merging of the learning resources and the classroom programs to a greater extent than ever before. Descriptions of existing patterns of organization, services, and arrangement and proposed guidelines, which can contribute to the systematic development of learning resources programs in relation to media innovation for instructional purposes are greatly needed.

Among the few materials which address the community college learning resources program and its relationship to the instructional program are citations (to be found in ERIC) of descriptions of single programs. B. Lamar Johnson has surveyed innovations in community college instruction but concentrated on the use of learning resources in the instructional program without dealing directly with their source—the community college's learning resources program.

An increasing number of institutions are developing a learning resources program. With the trend toward consolidation of print and nonprint services under the management of one person, community college administrators need information on program development, both successes and failures.

This book is intended to serve as a reference tool for community college program planners. Certain assumptions concerning both community college instructional and learning resources programs were made before collecting and analyzing the data and writing the book, as follows:

1. Community colleges are experiencing significant growth and will continue to do so for the foreseeable future.

2. Instruction is a primary objective of the community college program.

3. Learning resources programs exist, at least to some degree, in many community colleges.

4. The presence of a learning resources program can substantially improve or contribute to the improvement of the instructional program.

5. Learning resources programs are being rapidly and extensively developed by community college personnel on the basis of the prior four assumptions.

6. Little literature or research is readily available to support or guide the extension of learning resources programs being made in assumption number five.

7. Despite the lack of recorded information, reliable data can be gathered by contacting administrators, learning resources personnel, and professional association members.

8. There is no one way to use learning resources in conjunction with the community college's instructional program.

9. A group of knowledgable people with backgrounds and experience in learning resources and community college activities can validate a set of guidelines for use in the development of a learning resources program.

The steps in preparation of the book included collection of a variety of data about the current status of community college learning resources programs in relation to instructional practices, analysis and description of existing services, and development of guideline statements which will assist in the systematic design of learning resources programs. Promising practices in the organization and implementation of learning resources programs in community colleges have been identified, with special attention given to instructional practices perceived to be innovative by community college personnel.

Population identification, literature review, and questionnaire construction constituted first steps in data collection, followed by tabulation and analysis of questionnaire responses, a site visit to each of seven selected community colleges, and the construction of a set of concluding guideline statements illustrating practices and activities occurring in learning resources programs and instructional areas.

In order to make this a manageable and meaningful undertaking, certain limitations were established.

1. The study was confined to community colleges with learning resources programs.

2. The study made no value judgments concerning superiority of one learning resources program over another, or one institution over another.

3. There was no established pattern or standard against which the data were collected, measured, evaluated, or described other than the basic framework delineated in this investigation.

4. The study considered only those programs which were operational. Therefore, many interesting programs and facilities still in the developmental stages were excluded.

5. Only those colleges listed in the eighth edition of *American Junior Colleges*, which reported both print

and nonprint materials among their holdings, and those community colleges listed in the 1972 *Directory of State-Accredited Maryland Colleges and Universities* were selected as institutions to receive the initial questionnaire. (Not included in the study were learning resources programs in private and/or nonpublic community colleges.)

The focus is upon two-year public community colleges. Of the 827 possible colleges, 322 institutions met the two criteria which were used to identify the sampling population: (1) print and nonprint materials must be available in the learning resources collection, and (2) more than one thousand nonprint items in more than one format category must be in the collection.

After examining the descriptive information in *American Junior Colleges*, it was found that 487 of the 811 community colleges had both print and nonprint materials in their collections. After applying the second criterion, the survey population was reduced to 316 institutions. In studying the sixteen public two-year colleges in Maryland, it was discovered that ten were already included in the 316 institutions. The addition of the remaining six community colleges in Maryland brought the survey population to 322 public community colleges.

QUESTIONNAIRE

In order to survey the 322 selected institutions, a questionnaire (Appendix F) was designed. The design of the questionnaire was formulated after examining various studies which required the collection of similar information and by reviewing ideas and opinions found in the literature relating to community college instructional programs, innovation, and learning resources. The following studies and research projects were helpful: Mary V. Gaver, *Services of Secondary School Media Centers: Evaluation and Development*; James W. Liesener, *A Process for Planning School Media Programs: Defining Service Outputs, Determining Resource and Operational Requirements, and Estimating Program Costs*; Edna F. Hinman, *Checklist of Educational Innovation*; W. R. Fulton, *Evaluative Checklist: An Instrument for Self-Evaluating an Educational Media Program in Colleges and Universities*; and American Library Association and others, *Guidelines for Two Year College Learning Resources Programs*. The criteria for formulating the questions included (1) requested information not readily accessible from other sources and (2) information which was relevant to the investigation.

The data collected, described, and analyzed about learning resources programs in community colleges were based on the following questions.

1. Are print and nonprint services interrelated on community college campuses? If so, how are they related?

2. What proportion of community colleges use media to provide portions of the instructional program for individual learners (learning resources concept)?

3. What are the learning resources services provided in those community colleges using the learning resources concept?

4. What are the learning resources facilities in community colleges?

5. Which of the services provided directly facilitate instruction?

6. What are the responsibilities of the learning resources staff?

7. What are the patterns of administrative organization for community college learning resources services?

8. What are the patterns of development of learning resources programs in community colleges?

9. Are there patterns of development in relation to organization, facilities, and services which would optimize future community college learning resources program growth?

SITE VISITS

From an analysis of the survey data (responses from 150 usable questionnaires), seven institutions were selected for a site visit. The general characteristics used in selecting the institutions were (1) geographic distribution of location, (2) range of sizes of the student body and faculty members, (3) variety of instructional strategies, (4) differing services being provided by the learning resources programs, and (5) range of size and diversity of the collections.

Once the five general characteristics were applied to the 150 community colleges, specific criteria were developed for analyzing the programs.

1. The informational services at the community college must be organized around the learning resources center concept.

2. There must be a staff of at least four professionals and four supportive personnel excluding student assistants.

3. Ten or more services must be provided by the learning

resources center staff for both students and faculty.

4. There must be evidence that extensive use of learning resources can be found in at least three curricular areas within the community college program.

5. There must be a definite correlation between these three curricular areas and educational innovation.

The seven community colleges selected for the site visits were—

1. Bergen Community College, Paramus, New Jersey;

2. City College of San Francisco, San Francisco, California;

3. College of DuPage, Glen Ellyn, Illinois;

4. Florissant Valley Community College, St. Louis, Missouri;

5. Greenfield Community College, Greenfield, Massachusetts;

6. Lane Community College, Eugene, Oregon;

7. Prince George's Community College, Largo, Maryland.

A profile of each college can be found in Appendix J.

A guide was developed (Appendix H) to assist with the site visits. An interview was conducted with the person named in the questionnaire as being responsible for the learning resource center program. Other members of the learning resource center staffs also participated in the interview, as well as faculty members who were involved in innovative instructional practices, and college administrators. Time was spent discussing both the learning resource center program and the instructional program with students. Discussions with all these groups provided further data and insights into the operations of these selected institutions. The results of the site visits are provided in Chapter Six.

QUESTIONNAIRE DATA ANALYSIS

The data were analyzed in order to describe the development and implementation of learning resources services in community colleges with special attention being given to innovative instructional practices. The steps followed were to—

1. tabulate responses according to organization and administration of learning resources facility types;

2. compile, chart, and analyze responses to each question;

3. tabulate responses for several questions according to regional accrediting associations;

4. treat data as percentages and/or averages;

5. summarize data;

6. apply responses to questions raised on page 00.

SITE VISIT DATA ANALYSIS

Data collected during the seven site visits were analyzed to confirm or amplify the innovative practices found in learning resources programs in community colleges. Special attention was directed to instructional practices which involved the use of media. The steps followed were to—

1. compile and analyze responses to site visit questionnaire;

2. prepare a profile for each of the sites visited;

3. report data reflecting—
    a. type and organization of materials;
    b. administrative organization and procedures,
    c. staffing patterns,
    d. programs of service,
    e. extent of use,
    f. budgetary conditions, and
    g. relationship of learning resources program to the instructional program;

4. report responses according to similar and dissimilar items.

GUIDELINE DEVELOPMENT

In order to generate a set of concluding guideline statements which illustrate techniques and styles of cooperative program development between the learning resources program and instructional program, the data from the review of literature, questionnaires, and site visits were analyzed. The three steps followed were to—

1. compare similar responses from questionnaire and site visits;

2. compile items found in majority of responses;

3. categorize the guideline entries under the following headings:
   a.) General
   b.) Personnel
   c.) Functions
   d.) Public Relations
   e.) Instructional Development

GUIDELINE VALIDATION

The concluding guideline statements were sent to a panel of five experts (named later) for review. Four criteria were used to select the panel members. They were that the—

1. individual must currently be involved in the community college field;

2. individual must be recognized by his or her peer group as being an authority in the community college field (determined by having been recognized as a consultant and having published materials in the learning resources area);

3. individual must have had experience in planning and/or conducting learning resource programs or innovative instructional programs in two-year community colleges;

4. individual must be able to respond to the draft guidelines within three weeks' time from date of mailing.

The process followed in obtaining the panelists was to—

1. contact national learning resources associations for existing lists of consultants for learning resources programs in community colleges;

2. examine "Brief List of Consultants for Library Programs in Two-Year Colleges," June 1971, containing twenty-two names made available by the Library Administration Division of the American Library Association, and letter dated June 11, 1976, from Clint Wallington, who was then the Director of Research and Communications, Association for Educational Communications and Technology, containing five names.

3. examine *Education Index*, *Library Literature*, and *Resources in Education* (ERIC) to determine whether or not these individuals had published material relating to community college learning resources programs or instructional innovation (Thirteen individuals had published materials.);

4. select five individuals to serve as the panel of experts, taking into consideration geographical location and job responsibilities.

The five panelists were—

1. Joleen Boch
   Director of Library Services
   College of the Canyons
   Valencia, California

2. Boyd Bolvin, Associate Dean of
   Instruction: Learning Resources
   Bellevue Community College
   Bellevue, Washington

3. John H. Carmichael, President
   Westmoreland County Community College
   Youngwood, Pennsylvania

4. Dorothy T. Johnson, Coordinator
   Library Technology
   Cuyahoga Community College
   Cleveland, Ohio

5. James O. Wallace, Librarian
   San Antonio College
   San Antonio, Texas

The panelists were asked to respond to the concluding guideline statements (Appendix I) by checking the "Agree" or "Disagree" column. The statements were based upon the assumption that learning resources personnel were already providing services in the areas of accessibility of resources, reference or information referral, consultation/planning with faculty and students, and instruction in the use of the learning resources program. The panelists were then asked to provide comments to clarify their responses. The last page of the guideline statements provided the panelists the opportunity to add criteria which were not included in one of the five areas.

The above information provides the context within which this book is written. Without an understanding of this, the information contained in the following chapters will not be as useful or meaningful.

Chapter I
Characteristics of the Community and Junior College

Although many persons thought it to be impossible, and some persons even thought it not desirable, community colleges have developed into a vital part of the American educational system. It has required a lot of dreamers, planners, and innovators to take the best, the right, the workable, and make it commonplace in accordance with community needs. Community college planners and developers have been actively involved as change agents. Such change has required work, involved risk, and seldom offered clear or immediate advantages. There has been no one single program, structure, model, or method suitable for all; the only good program has and will be the one which will satisfy the needs of the community the college it is designed to serve. No one can make totally accurate predictions, but it seems safe to say that community colleges will continue to deliver educational services for students and that community college personnel will continue to serve as educational change agents.

The blending and careful merging of all types of learning resources into the college's instructional program is providing many new learning alternatives. There now exist almost unlimited capabilities for furthering one's learning opportunities through the use of resources and technological developments. Research, planning, and other developmental activities have produced a body of ideas and programs oriented to meeting many levels of student need through a combination of instruction and learning resources to be used independently and at his/her own pace by the student.

OVERVIEW OF THE COMMUNITY COLLEGE

Two-year colleges, both public and private, have been growing at an accelerating rate since the first public junior college, Joliet College in Joliet, Illinois, was founded in 1901. Emphasis has been upon teaching, counseling, community relations, open admissions, ease of accessibility, and instructional innovation. The literature continues to make note of the growth of community and junior colleges, and if the projections hold true, this will continue. The Carnegie Commission on Higher Education has predicted that between 230 and 280 new public community colleges will be needed by 1980. (3:35–39). However, recession and the decline in funds for construction has slowed this process, so this projection has not become a reality on schedule.

As for all institutions involved in postsecondary education, not everything has remained favorable for the growth of the community college field. Programs have been placed in a far more competitive environment than had they been in the sixties. Edmund J. Gleazer, Jr., President of the American Association of Community and Junior Colleges, claims that developmental education, occupational education, and other services considered by the community colleges to be among their distinctive offerings are being absorbed into the programs of a growing number of other educational institutions and agencies. Expansion of the community college has been slowed but far from halted. For so long as the college has continued to meet the demand for community-based and performance-oriented programs, student enrollment has been maintained and even increased.

The community college benefits the entire community in which it is located. The institution, its students, its faculty and staff all consume local products and services. Frequently the campus attracts real estate development and brings types of industry into an area which enhance property value. Due to the educational and cultural climate created, an influx of people to the area is also possible.

Edmund Gleazer has developed a profile of the community college comprised of the following thirteen common characteristics. A community college is—

1. part of a state plan for higher education;

2. receiving greater financial support from state funds;

3. established and operated under standards set at the state level;

4. establishing admissions policies which admit all students who can benefit from a program;

5. charging little or no tuition;

6. located in an area which allows a large commuting student population easy access;

7. offering a wide variety of technical and semi-professional programs;

8. implementing a comprehensive program of services;

9. providing service to aid undereducated students of post–high school age;

10. assisted by a state-level junior college board for coordination of planning, programs, and services and for

state aid;

11. represented in a state board or council for coordination with other institutions of higher education;

12. organized with its own separate and distinct district board, facilities, and budget;

13. initiated and controlled locally with sufficient state participation to maintain standards. (10:36–37)

Community colleges can no longer be characterized as mere extensions of high school programs or watered-down baccalaureate degree programs. Gleazer states that the community college should be expected to provide a wide variety of programs directed toward fulfilling individual needs, interests, and abilities. Programs should be provided for anyone who can benefit from them and at the lowest possible cost.

The purposes of the community college have been defined by a number of educators, among them Harlacher (13:3), Kelley and Wilbur (19:14), and Monroe (25:49–180). Six purposes which are common to all three of these listings are to offer (1) transfer programs, (2) occupational programs, (3) general education, (4) guidance and counseling, (5) community services, and (6) programs for the disadvantaged. Within the framework of these six program areas, the staff of each community college build in unique ideas, thus enabling the institution "to become a comprehensive community college." (8:4)

Many writers have documented the need for the community college to be community based, thus becoming a full partner in all of the community's educational activities. Dean Evans and Ross Neagley claim that the prime purpose of the community college is to make some form of higher and continuing education available to *all* people who can benefit from such programs. (7:216) The community college must serve all persons who live within its service area and must make learning experiences available at times which are convenient for the student. Constantly changing community needs, coupled with the changes affecting educational performance, practices, methods, and philosophy, must be reflected in the program.

According to statistics collected by the American Association of Community and Junior Colleges (AACJC), the number of colleges grew over a ten-year period, from 912 colleges in 1967 to 1,235 in 1977. Enrollment in these institutions increased from 1,671,440 to 4,309,984 students during the same decade. Enrollment figures represent a head count rather than a full time equivalency figure and include all students (full-time or part-time) taking courses for credit which led toward an associate degree, diploma, or certificate.

Community college students are as heterogeneous as the community in which the college is located; students on the community college campus are representative of the community and, so, closely resemble the student population of local high schools. A major difference is that the college students are somewhat older and more highly motivated, since community college attendance is not compulsory. Also, since little or no tuition is charged, there is a tendency for people from lower–middle class families to enroll in community colleges. AACJC figures indicate that women make up 51 percent of the student body. Minority students are estimated to number between 15 and 20 percent of the full-time enrollment at two-year colleges, according to the Department of Health, Education and Welfare's Office for Civil Rights. Data provided by the Bureau of the Census show that in 1976, 62 percent of the students were over the age of 21.

Although the number of people in the traditional college-going age range of 18 to 24 will continue to decline through

1980, community and junior colleges are expected to continue growing because they offer more community-based educational programs for women, minorities, and older students. According to AACJC, enrollment by those 35 years of age and older in two-year colleges has already increased 30 percent from 1974 to 1976. Projections provided by the National Center for Educational Statistics indicate that between 1975 and 1985, enrollment at community, junior, and technical institutions will increase by 48 percent, while enrollment at four-year colleges will increase at a 4 percent growth rate. Over half of the students enrolled in college for the first time in 1977 were attending a two-year college.

A fact sheet prepared by AACJC, titled *Types of Programs Offered in Two-Year Colleges*, identifies the following programs:

> *Community Education and Special Interest Programs.* Other major programs are offered for those students or community members interested in civic, cultural, or recreational courses not carrying academic credit toward a degree, diploma, or certificate. Specific programs are also designed for such groups as women returning to school, labor union members, senior citizens, and those seeking job upgrading skills. Developmental and remedial programs, most often in communication skills, are also offered at two-year colleges.
> *Transfer/Liberal Arts/College Parallel.* These programs are designed for students who plan to continue their postsecondary education at a four-year college or university. The programs are comparable to the first two years of a baccalaureate degree program and usually terminate in an associate degree.
> *Vocational/Occupational/Technical.* This category of programs includes training in such fields as data processing technologies; health services and paramedical

technologies, such as dental hygiene, medical records; engineering technologies, including automotive, diesel and welding programs; business and commerce technologies, including restaurant management, accounting, and communications; and public service technologies, such as recreation and social work, police and fire science programs. These programs are designed to lead directly to employment in a specific established or emerging field; such programs lead to a certificate, diploma, or associate degree.

During the 1960s enrollments in the vocational/occupational/technical programs began to grow. This was due in part to the offering of newly designed courses which were needed by the industrial/business community. According to AACJC figures in 1965, 13 percent of the student body were enrolled in an occupational program. However, by 1970 approximately 30 percent of the students attending two-year colleges were taking occupational courses. It is estimated that approximately thirteen hundred different programs are offered in this area.

Although enrollment has increased in the occupational areas, many two-year colleges are experiencing increased numbers of students taking humanities and general education courses. A number of these courses are being offered via local newspapers and television or radio stations.

There has been rapid growth in the number of persons taking community education courses which neither carry academic credit nor lead toward a degree or certificate. It is estimated that in 1976, 3.2 million people were participating in such community education services offered through a community college. These include cultural events; upgrading job skills; family planning; adult basic education; health care services; life-coping techniques; crafts; special awareness programs for women, senior citizens, and minorities; and physical fitness programs.

A profile of a typical community college student shows that she is over 35 years old, a woman, married, attends college on a part-time basis, comes from a less affluent home, and has parents with less education than those of students enrolled in four-year colleges or universities. Twenty-five percent of its students enroll in a two-year college because of lower tuition rates.

Over two-thirds of the first-time, full-time freshmen at two-year colleges claim they plan to go on to earn a bachelor's degree. However, data from the "National Longitudinal Study of the High School Class of 1972" indicates that only one-quarter of these enrolled in a two-year college by 1972 had, in fact, transferred to a four-year institution by 1974. Further documentation of this is provided by L. Steven Zwerling, of Staten Island Community College, who states that up to 75 percent of first-semester community college students declare their intention to be future transfer students, but only about one-third of these ever go on to a four-year college. Only 14 to 17 percent of these original community college aspirants to a B.A. or B.S. actually earn a degree. (32:234–235) Numerous reasons are given as to why such a small proportion of community college students actually do transfer to four-year institutions. Among these are the higher tuition, difficult location, inability to attend due to family responsibilities, and the need for full-time employment. Some say that they no longer find education to be relevant or necessary to fulfill long-term personal aspirations.

OVERVIEW OF THE LEARNING RESOURCES PROGRAM

The communtiy and junior college then is an educational institution which fills a great need. Its growing importance is reflected in the increase in the number of institutions and the number of students being provided learning opportunities according to their current needs. In light of this, traditional programs of library services alone are not adequate components of the learning program for the community college student.

As described in *The Two Year College and Its Students: An Empirical Report* (2), the relationship of the learning resources program to the institution and its instructional objectives is (1) to provide leadership and assistance in the development of instructional systems which employ effective and efficient means of accomplishing those objectives; (2) to provide an organized and readily accessible collection of materials and supportive equipment needed to meet institutional, instructional, and individual needs of students and faculty; (3) to provide a staff qualified, concerned, and involved in serving the needs of students, faculty, and community; and (4) to encourage innovation, learning, and community service by providing facilities and resources which will make them possible.

The development of the community college learning resources program is a fascinating story about which little is understood as it relates to other libraries. Having searched for self identity for the past seventy years, the community college library has at last emerged into a role of significance. What exactly are learning resources? Are they a physical place, a concept, instructional materials, a support service, or all of these? The learning resources program in fact must become more a concept than a physical place. There will always be a need for a central facility, but there is no reason why learning resources *activities* cannot take place in any number of settings found throughout the college's campus or, for that matter, throughout the community itself.

To some people, "learning resources" means an integration of various types of media into the instructional process, but the most enlightened concept of learning resources implies a *systematically* developed program which allows materials, equipment, and techniques to be effectively and efficiently used. This implies that the community college learning resources program is a subsystem of its parent institution (the system). As a subsystem, the learning resources program supports the college's overall goals, objectives, and purposes. In order to achieve this, the learning resources staff must be actively involved in planning and implementing the college's total program.

This involvement includes the design of programs and an allocation of resources which will achieve program objectives and, in turn, modify and improve those activities which need change. This requires the use of all available and applicable planning techniques, extensive involvement of those affected, and mechanisms for monitoring and coordinating program activities. In order to survive and grow, a program must be able to monitor itself, evaluate its performance, and upgrade wherever or whenever needed.

Through the years, various sets of national standards have been written for community college libraries. In 1930 the American Association of Junior Colleges adopted a set of standards which were used until 1940. (23:20) The Association of College and Research Libraries, a division of the American Library Association, released its standards for junior and community colleges in 1960. These standards moved part way toward emphasis on the quality of materials, services, and staff as compared with quantity of items. In 1972, three national organizations (the American Library Association, the American Association of Community and Junior Colleges, and the Association for Educational Communications and Technology) jointly released the *Guidelines for Two-Year College Learning Resources Programs*. The emphasis has evolved so that it is squarely upon the quality of program and not on the facility where the resources are housed. The standards are diagnostic and descriptive in nature and were designed to give direction to community college personnel in the development of comprehensive learning resources programs. Evaluative criteria and information about community college libraries are now contained in the standards of the regional accrediting associations.

The importance of the learning resources center concept began to emerge in the late sixties; however, its acceptance has come hard. In searching the literature, one finds that the community college learning resources concept and program has been one of the most neglected of all areas of librarianship. Little documentation can be found, the basic professional tools omit this area, and the standards prior to 1972 provide little assistance in the development of the community college learning resources program. Richard Ducote, Dean of Learning Resources, College of DuPage in Illinois, provides several reasons why it has been difficult to formulate the concept of learning resources and services: (1) the diversity in purpose and the size of various institutions; (2) the large number of commuting students; (3) the varying course offerings; (4) the willingness of the administration to experiment; and (5) the variety found within the student body. (6:1)

As long as the community college shared facilities and staff with a high school, as many did in the beginning, the extent of library services to the college student was so limited that services addressing individual needs were nearly nonexistent. Before 1950, the two-year colleges had fairly traditional print-oriented collections with almost no nonprint items. During the 1950s community colleges began to discover that traditional library methods, practices, and materials were not meeting the needs of their students. Hours of service had to be expanded to include evenings, weekends, and summer sessions; total reliance on the services of another library could not be continued. The community college library was soon to be given the opportunity to develop independently and create its own facilities, but learning resources staff possessing the necessary training, competencies, and experiences were scarce.

B. Lamar Johnson has discovered that in the early sixties

a sizable number of community colleges were expanding materials collections to include various types of audiovisual aids. He suggests that many patrons were enjoying the benefits of "one-stop" shopping for instructional materials services. These materials were being used by instructors to facilitate the teaching process and by students to enhance their learning.

Federal support for community college learning resources has been available for nearly twenty years. Title I of the Higher Education Act of 1963 specified that 22 percent of all construction funds must be allotted to public community colleges and technical institutes. The Higher Education Act of 1965 provided additional monies for the purchase of materials which aided in the improvement of college instruction and counseling services.

In the increasing number of institutions which are now developing a learning resources program, changes have occurred throughout the college—from the administration to the community user. Faculty have discovered new and innovative ways for including various instructional resources in their courses of study. Students have discovered that the learning resources center can be an exciting and worthwhile place for all sorts of learning activities. The use of learning resources will continue to provide access to necessary information, helping persons make well-informed decisions from alternative possibilities. The capability of media to humanize and tailor learning and to reinforce interpersonal activity must be emphasized over the technological aspects of the media. Technology will continue, used in the right ways, to open up learning opportunities.

It is services which make learning resources programs a means toward educational excellence. Creative and innovative personnel must demonstrate and illustrate the media's linkage to the total educational process. One context for examining services is provided in the following broad categories. These five service components and descriptive statements provide a structure in which learning resources program activities can be examined:

Accessibility of Resources. A major responsibility of the learning resources staff is to make available all the center's holdings to the user with as few restrictions as possible. Materials included in the collection must reflect the varied interests, needs, levels of achievement, and learning styles—ranging from the gifted/talented to the physically/emotionally impaired. A wide variety of print and nonprint media must be provided.

Reference or Information Services. The learning resources staff must be skilled in helping users to locate information which answers their inquiries. Guidance in the selection of materials for leisure reading or viewing are important areas of learning resources program services. The staff must be aware of and able to tap into information referral activities, local/regional/statewide and multi-state networks.

Instruction. The learning resources staff has the responsibility to instruct students and faculty members in the use of the learning resources program, and must be able to apply the principles of learning and learning theory to a variety of instructional activities. Learning resources staff members serve as members of instructional teams responsible for designing and providing learning experiences.

Production of Media. Learning resources staff must be skillful in planning and producing a wide array of audiovisuals which support the teaching-learning process.

Consultation. Frequent consultations with other college personnel are a necessity, if the learning resources program is to develop in line with college needs and objectives. Together, the faculty and the learning resources staff can examine the affect resources and services are having upon student learning. This will assure the existence of a program which is supportive of the college's instructional program.

A learning resources program which is truly part of the college's instructional program will provide for rich inquiry and discovery experiences in support of learning activities. Media are the liberating factor which makes possible the widest sharing of human experiences through the senses as well as through the mind.

Chapter II
Learning Resources and Instruction

Leaders in the community college field stress the mutual enhancement of learning resources programs and classroom instruction when there is close linkage between the two. The learning resources program must become a catalytic agent which spurs and encourages instructors to use the creative teaching practices which ensure greater student learning opportunities. Only when equipped with the widest range of materials can the learning resources program serve this role. The library cannot be thought of as containing only print materials just as media cannot be thought of as meaning solely nonprint materials. In today's learning resource centers all educational communications technology must be merged into one functional program. Community colleges have led the way for other libraries in combining print and nonprint resources, thus creating a learning resources center program. Supporting *all* instructional activities and satisfying the informational needs (formal and informal, curriculum-related and personal) of the community college student is the major function of the learning resources program.

Because the community college learning resources program supports classroom instruction so closely, its staff becomes involved not only in the preparation of materials, the furnishing of equipment, and the operation of autotutorial laboratories, but also in the actual classroom teaching. In this respect the community college learning resources program staff differs greatly from that of other academic libraries, since most academic librarians are not directly involved in providing instructional activities other than library skills and orientation sessions.

There was little incentive to emphasize learning resources or encourage independent student use as long as instruction focused on the single textbook concept and lectures were the standard one-way means for imparting information from instructor to student. This is changing. Many community college teachers are using an abundance of educational technology in classroom instruction to stimulate exchange and interaction. Learning resources centers, amply supplied with materials and equipment, are becoming as universal as traditional college libraries once were; their value can only be measured in terms of their responsiveness in fulfilling the needs of the individual users. The learning resources program must have access to all types of informational sources which will assist learning, not just those held in its own facility.

The role of the community college's learning resources staff members has been studied by many groups. The most recent comprehensive study can be found in *Career Patterns of Community College Librarians*, a 1973 doctoral study by S. A. Edsall. The learning resources staff must be thoroughly familiar with both the theories and applications of learning styles and curriculum development, as well as with all types of learning materials. The staff must have the competencies and skills to work with individual students and also with groups of students who have different cultural backgrounds, abilities, and educational needs. Knowledge of the history, philosophy, objectives, and educational potential of community colleges as a group is also helpful. Unlike most academic librarians, the learning resources staff were recognized as early as the middle fifties as members of the instructional staff and were assigned to

work with the faculty of various departments. (15:229)
However, the ultimate responsibility for greater involvement of the learning resources staff with the instructional
program falls upon the college administration. Administrators must first hold to a firm expectation of such involvement and then must seek out and hire those individuals who
are competent and enthusiastic about reentering the classroom and becoming involved in instructional development
activities. When these two things occur, the learning
resources staff can no longer be viewed as an appendage to
the college's instructional program, engaged in an optional
or supplementary program.

There must also develop a mutual understanding, cooperation, and respect as to complementary roles in the instructional process between the learning resources staff and all
instructors. This should include knowledge of one another's
constraints, limitations, bureaucratic/administrative red
tape, and a concerted effort to assess the needs and capabilities of the student body. All learning resources personnel
should become involved in instruction outside of, as well as
inside, the center itself, going into the classroom to teach a
unit on library usage, an entire course on bibliographic/
library research, or any other course they are qualified to
teach. It may perhaps be difficult, but the rewards will be
great if a peripheral or under-utilized facility becomes a
beehive of activity and an integral part of the learning
process.

Fusaro projects the idea that it is time for all of the
nation's community colleges not only to develop the learning resources program concept but to move toward the
implementation of the full library-college concept. (9:44)
Language laboratories, study skill centers, television
studios, dial access and other systems can provide students
expanded opportunities for independent learning. There is a
growing tendency for all learning laboratories to be administered as a unit of the learning resources program. Since the

true learning resources program provides learning activities which have been jointly prepared by instructors and learning resources personnel, the students can work at their own pace to develop skills and acquire needed knowledge.

There is a need for curricular innovation in community college instructional practices. This need is heightened by an increased number of students seeking quality preparation in order to transfer to university programs; new demands being produced by technological advances; and taxpayer revolts and the resulting focus on operational efficiency. As an integral part of the college's instructional program, the learning resources program must provide leadership for the development, coordination, dissemination, and evaluation of information which assists in student learning. All components of these programs must be constructed around the institution's philosophy, goals, and objectives; the objectives of the students and faculty; and the needs of the larger community.

The blending of all types of learning resources into the community colleges' instructional programs provides many new learning alternatives. Research and technology have produced a cadre of ideas and programs directed to meeting learner needs. However, care must be taken to ensure that the learning resources program does not run parallel to the instructional program instead of merging with it. A strong and positive program of learning services, cooperatively developed by the subject-teaching faculty and learning resources program staff, can ensure a successful combination.

Classroom instruction and learning resources should both be viewed as subsystems of the college, and their interrelationships purposefully established through the college's master plan. Curricular development that involves learning resources staff and services from the onset must be a component in the college's overall planning process. As the master plan is developed and supporting instructional programs outlined and presented, data which validate the role for the learning resources program and its overall effectiveness in helping the college fulfill its mission should be continually collected and integrated into the feedback and evaluation process. The master plan should serve two overall purposes. It should—

1. provide a means whereby the community, staff, and students are made aware of the mission, goals, objectives, and directions of the college over a given period of time; and

2. assist college personnel in allocating resources (personnel, budgetary, materials/equipment, and facilities) for accomplishing the activities and purposes as stated in the plan.

In the vast body of literature on planning, there are numerous models, statements, and structures around which a master plan should be developed. Here is one model which provides a clear and concise outline for the various components to be included in a master plan:

Mission and Purpose. The mission is a broad, philosophical statement reflective of the entire role of the college; purposes are broad statements highlighting major parts of the mission statement.

Goals and Priorities. Goals should be stated as outcomes of the desired results for each of the purposes; priorities refer to the value or relative importance, in descending order, of each goal.

Problems and Solutions. This portion of the plan represents those problems perceived by staff, students, and community members and their potential solutions. Before arriving at solutions, a number of alternatives need to be formulated, and the most appropriate one selected for solving the problem.

Historical and Future Data. These are data concerning the past and future that are collected for use in the development of objectives and programs.

Objectives and Programs. Objectives and programs are the specific, measurable objectives that are arrived at through the synthesis of goals and priorities, problems and solutions, and historical and future data. (22:5–6)

When the plan is completed, it will serve as a guide for the operation of the college during the time span for which it is written. It will also show the interrelationships among all units within the college and provide direction for meaningful interplay between the instructional program and learning resources. The plan will enable the learning resources program to better fulfill its instructional and support service by informing users of its overall role.

Curriculum can be defined as a set of planned learning activities, sequentially arranged, which, when completed, will have enabled the student to learn a new skill or to experience a change in behavior, or both. Numerous internal and external forces will impact the process before the learning activity is actually completed. A systems approach to instructional design will facilitate learning improvement when such an approach is based upon measurable institutional objectives. Figure 1 provides a graphic illustration of the instructional design or development process.

Instructional design or development is the term given to the process which helps ensure that learning occurs as the end product of a system. Neither the term nor the process is new, but many persons still do not understand the purpose, process, or results of this type of instructional planning. Properly used, the process requires the involvement of all persons who will share the responsibility for providing the

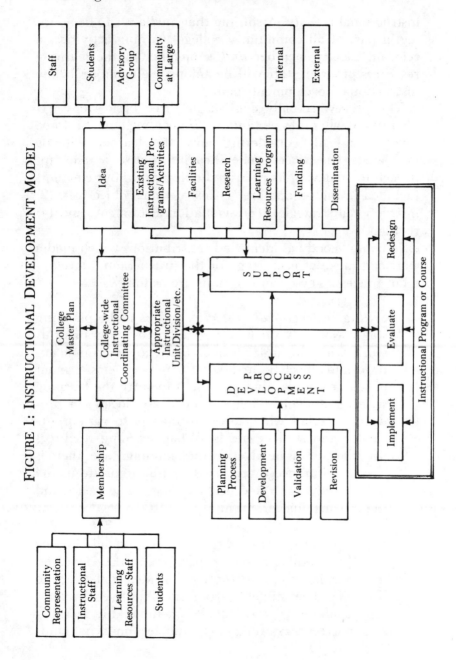

FIGURE 1: INSTRUCTIONAL DEVELOPMENT MODEL

instructional activity. Assuming that media are to be an integral part of all community college learning activities, a
relevant faculty member *and* a member of the learning
resources program staff will be among the members of the
instructional development team.

The process actually consists of three basic steps: (1)
identifying what is to be taught, (2) deciding how it is to be
taught, and (3) considering how the learner will be
evaluated. The process relies heavily upon a systems approach to achieving its prestated objectives. Four elements
included in the process are (1) instructional objectives, (2)
instructional strategies, (3) evaluation/assessment, and (4)
revision.

Johanna Wood has identified contributions which media
staff can make at each stage of the instructional development process. These contributions are as follows:

> *Setting Instructional Objectives.* This is the planning
> stage. Not only do learning resources program staff
> work with the instructional team to determine ap-
> propriate objectives arrived at through the assessment
> of learner needs, they also help identify the learning
> styles of students. They can purchase, locate, or pro-
> duce materials which are appropriate to varied cur-
> ricular and student needs. When learning resources
> program staff is involved at the planning stage, there is
> greater assurance that varied and appropriate media
> will be fully integrated into the learning sequence and
> the instructional program.
>
> *Constructing Learning Activities.* It is equally impor-
> tant that learning resources program staff be involved
> in determining the instructional strategies that are to
> be used to help students attain the objectives. In plan-
> ning conferences with faculty members the learning
> resources center staff can help to determine what kinds

of media are best suited for those specific instructional strategies which will utilize media. Additionally, assistance can be provided to the faculty member in the production of media, such as transparencies, learning activity packages, mediated instructional modules, filmstrips, slide-tape presentations, and other media formats.

Evaluating/Assessing the Outcomes of Instruction. Ongoing evaluation is essential to sound instructional development. It is important that the evaluation plan be performance-based in relation to the instructional objectives. Learning resources program staff can help gather data and analyze feedback about student progress through the use of such methods as observation and interaction with students. This data will reinforce the results of performance testing and provide the instructional team with the means to determine if the individual learners are achieving the objectives.

Revising the Instructional Program. If the objectives are not being achieved by learners, then it is necessary to select alternative strategies and media that the learners can use. It is the feedback part of the evaluation loop that provides for the revision of the instructional plan if the learners have not achieved the objectives. The learning resources center staff then assists in the identification of alternative learning activities and appropriate media.

Together, the faculty members and the learning resources program staff examine the effect media are having upon student learning. This helps to assure that the collection of resources and learning activities are really addressing the college's needs.

It must be noted that, being humans, both the learning

resources staff and the faculty will want to be satisfied that their particular interests are protected before cooperative activities will take place easily, naturally, and as a matter of course. It will probably take several years of close, direct interaction before anything like a college-wide "habit" can be achieved. Almost all studies indicate that successful teamwork and a change in the instructional development process seem to require several years of effort before the practice becomes commonplace. Of course, there are those exceptional persons who have already been initiated into the potentials of planning cooperatively or who are especially quick to grasp the benefits of such teamwork. Since these individuals are apt to be leaders in other ways, too, they can sell the idea to others. Administrators also occupy a crucial role in supporting the use of learning resources. Utilization occurs when the involved staff perceive such to be in their best interest and in the interest of those providing leadership and serving as authority figures.

The diverse student body and wide range of learning abilities found in the community colleges make the selection and development of teaching strategies and learning materials especially critical. If learning is really to take place, students must become totally involved in the instructional process — from the design stage on. The learning resources staff must facilitate and encourage this involvement. The right choice of alternatives is a most crucial element. Faculty members may reflect, direct, suggest, and, when necessary, perhaps, even order, to ensure that choices known about are considered and carefully selected. It is incumbent upon faculty members that they understand the needs and interests of all students and how they learn. The community college has recognized as a way of life, a given, that it is the student around whom the instructional program is organized.

Let it be firmly stated and fully understood that no mode of presentation of curricular material relieves the instructor of the responsibility for integrating into a course the instructional objectives, teaching procedures, and means for evaluating student progress. Learning resources, including all media used in the instructional process and the necessary equipment for their proper use, will contribute little to the quality of instruction unless the resources are selected carefully by the instructor to fit a specific learning situation. Learning resources extend, expand, are an intrinsic part of teaching strategies; they do not substitute for them. Teaching is a technology in which a set of ideas to be communicated is combined with a set of instructional activities which are designed for student learning.

Ralph W. Tyler lists ten conditions which are essential for learning:

1. The learner must have an opportunity to carry on the new behavior.

2. He/she must find satisfaction in carrying it on.

3. He/she must be able to practice the new behavior until it becomes part of his/her available repertoire of behavior.

4. He/she must be self-motivated.

5. He/she must realize that his/her old ways of behavior are inferior to the new ones.

6. He/she needs guidance so that the learning period can be shortened.

7. He/she must have time for practice.

8. He/she needs to practice the learned behavior in a sequential context so that earlier behavior can be used in

a new situation which provides greater depth, complexity, and understanding.

9. He/she needs standards which are high for him/her but also attainable.

10. He/she needs feedback or evidence of the rate of learning progress so that motivation can be maintained. (25:275)

Learning then becomes a process in which technology, resources, and the instructor are brought together, with each functioning in a complementary way in relation to the others. Technology may take over many of the routine chores of teaching, continuously evaluate individual progress, and provide quick access to data. Learning resources can bring the world into the classroom, reinforcing verbal abstractions with concrete picture and sounds. The instructor, leading and guiding students on an individual and small-group basis, integrates and paces the other elements.

According to Kelley and Wilbur, who have confirmed with research what common sense dictates anyway, knowledge of subject matter, media, and techniques is not enough to make for effective teaching. The manner in which information is presented and the ways in which a variety of material is incorporated into the instructional process must be considered, too. One's mannerisms, imagination, and personality combined with teaching strategies assist in determining teacher effectiveness. It is the interaction with resources and with students, and instructional style, that account for differences in learning effectiveness. It is likely that a really good teacher will make any program or activity effective.

There are three major factors which characterize the teaching/learning process at the college level: (1) students can voluntarily choose the instructional program; (2)

students make judgments about the content and quality of instruction received, judgments which, in turn, influence the voluntary choices made; and (3) students have motivation to learn. Most community college instructors are adequately trained to teach their subjects. However, problems do occur because most instructors are middleclass and may tend to devalue occupational programs and educational programs for the disadvantaged. Lowerclass attitudes often conflict with the faculty members' value code of hard work, diligence, and conformity to college rules and regulations. The gap between instructor and student can be bridged with understanding and the realization that human beings possess different abilities and that alien behavior can be learned. It must be assumed that instruction in the future will be more learner-centered, individual-oriented, and community-based.

Teaching methods and techniques have been expanded dramatically with the acceptance of alternatives to the formal lecture approach. Thousands of experiments have been conducted dealing with teaching methods. Many of the experiments report no significant difference in results between the experimental process and a more traditional one. Students and faculty generally do feel a great degree of satisfaction in participating in the experiments, but the results, as measured by standardized tests, do not assign a particular advantage to one method over another. Even though outcomes or products are difficult to interpret, the evidence to date is not encouraging to those who would hope that a single, reliable, multipurpose teaching strategy could be used with confidence. In *Models of Teaching*, Joyce presents a number of teaching models and analyzes them in terms of their implications for curriculum design, for instructors working with students, and for the development of instructional materials. (18)

One difficulty with instructional/teaching research lies in the fact that excessive time has been spent looking at variables which have secondary importance to learning. This is the reason that most studies which study one method and use a control group for purposes of comparison find no significant differences — for example, between television instruction and live instruction; between large-class lecturing and small-class lecturing; between textbook reading and programmed instruction. In fact, there are variables which might have greater influence on the findings: (1) environment, (2) task, and (3) individual differences.

The Research and Policy Committee of the Committee for Economic Development has stated that innovation in education, in the form of new curriculum materials or educational technology, is essential if education is to be fully effective in achieving established goals and objectives. Community colleges which desire to remain vital educational institutions must continue to experiment with innovative practices, but numerous studies and reports indicate that resistance to innovation and change is deeply embedded. Havelock, among others, has identified six steps which an individual must go through before an innovative practice is accepted: (1) awareness, (2) interest, (3) evaluation, (4) trial, (5) adoption, and (6) integration. (14:113) There is such a leisurely diffusion rate for educational innovation, that once an idea has been projected which might fill a need or solve an existing problem, it will take approximately fifty years for complete acceptance. (24:51) It appears that most innovative methods have been introduced quite rightly for the purpose of improving instruction. While some innovations have been found to provide financial savings, this consideration alone should not be sufficient reason for the adoption of any practice. Many new methods of instruction provide the kind of flexibility that will be of ever-increasing importance, although, of course, the effectiveness of new methods must be assessed in terms of cost/benefit ratios as students assume greater involvement in their own education.

Innovation which is easily institutionalized is more likely

to receive acceptance, it is found, than that which requires creativity, cannot be routinely managed, or presents too great a threat to existing practices. The success of any change agent is positively related to the extent to which that agent is initiated through opinion leaders, those who are more willing than others to take risks based upon their past success and status among peers.

Innovation is difficult to define except in relative terms, for what constitutes innovation in one institution may be common practice in another. In order for innovation to occur, the institution must consciously develop a conducive environment, one in which faculty members are encouraged to try new methods which may improve their teaching styles.

Since the primary mission of the community college is to serve local needs, and because of the rapid rate at which changes occur locally, curriculum development and its implementation must be thought of as a circular process — one which has a beginning but which has no end. All instructors must be given not only the encouragement but the tools with which to be inventive people who will continuously discover new ways of doing things. Today's community and junior colleges are providing their instructors with the instructional resources and equipment which innovative practices require. Materials, in all formats and at varying levels of difficulty, provide every instructor with the opportunity to extend teaching effectiveness.

All instructors must discover methods by which they can express themselves and their subject matter to address the needs of their students. To do this, they must be helped to experiment with new approaches and to adapt those that suit them. Because it is not restrained by long-standing traditions nor an elitist student philosophy, the community college has unprecedented opportunities to strike out in new directions in all areas of teaching and learning. The effective use of materials can be of enormous help in its development. Learning resource programs will help to reinforce the high correlation between a faculty member's belief that even the least motivated and most difficult student can learn, and the learning rate which actually occurs within the community college.

Chapter III
Staff Development

Although community college personnel generally have become aware of the essential role of the learning resources program in the work of their students, there is some difficulty in all community colleges in getting learning resources fully integrated into the instructional program. Without this integration, the full value of the learning resources program is unrealized. When the instructional program and the learning resources program are totally merged, one can find a cost-effective justification for program growth and expansion.

The professional staff of the learning resources program must be trained as teachers as well as library information specialists. The competencies required of them are far more varied and extensive than were those expected of the traditional librarian or audiovisual specialist. The skills required of them, as of all community college personnel, are reflecting the rapid growth and change in this part of America's educational system. In addition to the shared responsibility we have discussed for instructional design, there are new management systems, changing technology, plant maintenance, and operation to be mastered, as well as ever greater variation in the interests and needs presented by the student body.

The quality of the learning resources program is measured in terms of its materials, staff, and services, and also the degree to which it helps to achieve the community college's instructional goals. The end product is improved learning and a major role in the fulfillment of the college's accountability program.

More and more faculty members are expecting a host of learning materials to help them do their jobs better. To these professionals, the issue is not if or why materials should be used in teaching, but *how* materials can and should be used to improve teaching and learning. As more faculty members incorporate new techniques and materials into their classroom activities, and the learning resources program staff is expected to support them in these activities, the critical issue facing community college designers, planners, and developers is how and where to find personnel who can do the job. Since preservice educational programs can not fully meet this challenge, locally designed and implemented staff development programs have become mandatory. The development and implementation of sound staff development programs will have a major impact on educational opportunities; lack of them can be disastrous.

For several decades, a dedicated handful of people has been insisting on the need for staff development to improve the effectiveness of the performance of all personnel — be they full- or part-time; faculty, clerical, or technical staff; administrators, governing board members, or advisory committee members. In light of the needs, it is frequently tempting to accept the mandate and proceed, often in too single-minded a manner and without sufficient planning. In doing so, a major concern may be overlooked, the opportunity to strengthen the relationships among staff development, instructional development, and institutional development. The three cannot run separate courses but must be combined into one totally integrated plan. This integrated approach will enable the community college to examine the compatibility of activities with the objectives being sought and enable the institution to provide staff development programs which will not only increase the performance, competency level, and effectiveness of each employee, but also benefit the overall institution in many ways. While all staff development activities should focus upon the training, development, and resources which affect behavior, attitudes, beliefs, values, and skills of all the staff, they should do so in terms of increasing staff ability to assist in achieving the college's overall mission.

Staff development can be equated with change — both personal and institutional. The activities, in order to be effective, must be participatory and provide meaningful experience. Although staff development activities in community colleges are fairly new, experiences found in other fields can provide insights and direction.

Educational Testing Service released in November 1976 a study of staff development programs in 326 two-year colleges by John A. Centra. The findings show that 49 percent of the colleges had a unit or person responsible for staff development or instructional improvement. The median life span of these units to that date was only 2.5 years. Fifty-six percent of the colleges had single full-time directors, 14 percent had two or three full-time staff, and 18 percent, four or more staff assigned to staff development activities. (27:11)

The organization, management, and coordination of the staff development program should be assigned to a staff development unit within the community college. The size of the college and the number and depth of program offerings will dictate the size of the development program staff. The head of the program should have status and rank with all other administrative staff members with similar responsibilities. The program staff need to be familiar with the available resources of the college and the community; without this knowledge the staff development program cannot provide learning experiences geared to the needs of the people it is designed to serve.

Those responsible for the staff development program

must formulate a sequence of activities which are planned, announced, and made available to all who want or need to enroll. The development of the activities should be a shared responsibility, with each person assigned a task to be completed; frequently an advisory committee for staff development is a useful instrument.

Since a number of community colleges have instructional development specialists assigned to the learning resources program and since learning to design and improve instruction is a major component of a good staff development program, coordination between learning resources and staff development programs should be worked out in order to insure that the two are supporting each other's activities. Furthermore, the resources (materials, equipment, staff, and facilities) of the learning resources program will be essential to the staff of the development program.

An examination of the literature on staff development shows that there are many components that are considered important. However, not all of them are essential for success, nor does their inclusion guarantee success. There is little agreement as to how staff development activities should be structured. The only absolute is that the program must reflect both institutional and personal needs, but how this is to be accomplished must be left to the creative ingenuity of staff development planners, designers, and implementers found in each community college.

Advice drawn from the literature includes the following:

1. Assess needs of all employees through both formal and informal — such as a questionnaire and an exchange of ideas in discussion—means.

2. Provide experiences which involve participants in everything from planning to evaluation, according to their specific needs, and enable them to provide positive changes in the quality of instruction.

3. Offer opportunities which provide a balance between theory and practice, are linked to college-wide efforts, and are part of an overall strategy or plan;

4. Facilitate the diffusion of learned skills throughout the institution.

5. Plan for appropriate balance in benefits composed of professional training, personal development, and institutional growth. The focus is not on initial educational experience but upon retaining and renewal of skills and competencies needed to perform one's job requirements.

6. Provide support by the community college in terms of fiscal, personnel, facility, material, and programmatic resources. Release time from scheduled assignments is a *must*.

7. Offer a comprehensive program of activities with objectives that are stated in terms of behavioral outcomes and evaluated accordingly. The participants will function best if they know what is expected prior to undertaking an activity.

8. Provide opportunities which are not readily available through or included in preservice education. Preservice programs and inservice/continuing education should be cooperatively designed and carried out as a continuous, ongoing process and not, as is too often the case, two mutually exclusive experiences. The need for constant upgrading of job-related skills makes inservice/continuing education programs as necessary and important as preservice education.

9. Include opportunities for demonstration, role playing,

simulation, discussion, hands-on experiment, and other means of "trying out" new learning and behaviors rather than requiring participants to save new knowledge for use at a later time.

10. Facilitate effective interaction between presenters, participants, the college, and the community.

11. Offer activities in various settings and through a variety of presentation styles which will address participants' needs, such as:
    a. seminars or institutes
    b. designing and developing learning materials
    c. workshops, inservice sessions, or retreats
    d. formal courses leading to advanced degrees
    e. individually designed modules
    f. independent study
    g. research activities
    h. work experiences in different settings
    i. planned visits to other community colleges or appropriate institutions/agencies
    j. attendance/participation at local, state, and national conferences
    k. writing articles/books pertaining to areas of interest and expertise
    l. desk conferences
    m. serving on committees engaged in activities which advance the goals and directions of the college

Competence is the demonstrated ability to accomplish a task, activity, or project either by oneself or with others. Competencies involve the simultaneous interplay of knowledge, skill or ability, understanding, positive attitudes, and constructive values. It is necessary for each individual to examine continually the competencies needed in order to per-

form successfully on the job, for the competencies required
of all community college personnel today are far more
varied and extensive than were those expected of past
employees. New methods, including technology and content, all require retraining of existing personnel and provide
further substantiation, as if any were needed, for systematically planned and designed staff development programs.

The American Association of Community and Junior Colleges identified staff development as a priority program in
the late 1960s. The Association has sponsored summer
workshops, a national assembly, numerous seminars and
conferences to discuss and implement college inservice
development efforts, and released several publications. In
the spring of 1977 the AACJC provided further impetus
with its development of the National Council for Staff, Program and Organizational Development (NCSPOD). Prior
to the formation of NCSPOD, four regional meetings were
held to explore its feasibility, direction, and purposes. A
national meeting, sponsored by the Fund for the Improvement of Postsecondary Education, through a grant provided
to Burlington County College, New Jersey, provided a
meeting ground for those interested in the creation of the
Council. In January 1978, AACJC formally approved its
affiliation with NCSPOD. Today the Council has nearly
five hundred members representing more than thirty of the
fifty states; its purpose is to foster staff, program, and
organizational development in public and private two-year
community, junior, and technical colleges throughout the
United States. Specifically, the goals and objectives are—

1. to foster innovative and effective approaches to staff,
   program, and organizational development;

2. to foster means for self-development of persons interested in staff, program, and organizational develop-

ment;

3. to maintain communication among offices and organizations concerned with staff, program, and organizational development;

4. to foster research and evaluation in the field of staff, program, and organizational development.

NCSPOD offers a broad range of services and activities focusing upon community college staff development opportunities. Among these services and activities are:

1. resource development
2. research and dissemination
3. a human resource directory
4. a national newsletter
5. a national forum via conference, regional meetings, and assistance to state organizations

In the area of staff development, the Council has dealt primarily with leadership, management, faculty, and classified employee development. Program development is concerned with assessing community program needs and designing, supporting, and evaluating programs. Improving the power and effectiveness of two-year colleges through the use of goals and mission-setting techniques, team-building activities, change processes, systems theory, and intervention strategies are among the concerns of the organizational development area. (26)

Both the Association and the Council have been successful in providing leadership and focus to community college staff development activities. Both have made it possible for the colleges to explore alternatives for ensuring that a competent staff, effective programs, and functional organizations exist so that college personnel can more effectively accomplish their work assignments.

Although it is next to the impossible for even the most ex-perienced practitioners to reach consensus on what should be included in staff development activities, it is possible to examine the process which can be used in organizing a pro-gram that addresses both personal and institutional needs. Composed of those same elements used in any structuring effort, the process includes planning, conducting, and evaluating. These components do not, of course, stand alone; there is much overlap. The process is circular and continuing, with revision and restructuring built into it.

PLANNING THE PROGRAM

It must be made clear and believable from the start that the staff development activity is to be positive and un-threatening. Planning a staff development program must be viewed as a team effort, geared to providing motivation and supervisory support and involving each participant in self-development.

Planning includes the processes of assessing needs, identi-fying opportunities, analyzing problems, establishing prior-ities, selecting activities, and allocating available resources (personnel, materials, facilities, budget, and time). It is necessary because it gives direction and perspective to all ac-tivities. Planning facilitates the involvement of concerned people or groups, provides for effective communications, and makes possible coordination among the various ac-tivities which make up a staff development program.

All staff development activities should be incorporated into a planned program — a program being a group of ac-tivities which have been combined into a structure and are carried out to achieve some previously stated objectives. (See Figure 2 for Staff Development Model.)

First is the need to assess the personal, instructional and

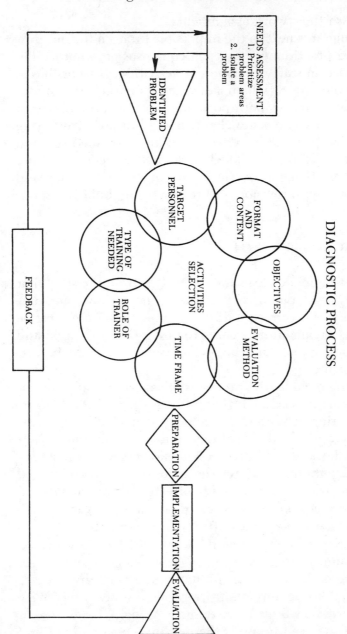

NEEDS ASSESSMENT
1. Prioritize
   problem areas
2. Isolate a
   problem

IDENTIFIED PROBLEM

DIAGNOSTIC PROCESS

TARGET PERSONNEL

FORMAT AND CONTENT

TYPE OF TRAINING NEEDED

ACTIVITIES SELECTION

OBJECTIVES

ROLE OF TRAINER

TIME FRAME

EVALUATION METHOD

FEEDBACK

PREPARATION

IMPLEMENTATION

EVALUATION

FIGURE 2

STAFF DEVELOPMENT MODEL

institutional needs of the community college staff and the college itself. The assessment process includes both formal and informal data-gathering activity using questionnaires and interviews; searching through existing documents; examining local, state and national trends; and relying upon one's own intuition and experience for direction. Once the assessment has been completed, areas for inclusion in the staff development program can be identified and priorities established from among the most critical. The list of opportunities identified will be far more exhaustive than can probably be undertaken initially. Because this is so, each of the opportunities or indications of need will require further analysis. Especially important to this process will be the consideration and, if necessary, the formation of institutional goals and objectives which relate specifically to staff development. Priorities will have to be established also which relate to the availability of resources and interrelationships between the staff development program and other college functions and programs.

Activities will have to be selected which will enable participants from all segments of the college staff to engage in experiences that will help them advance their skills. The program of activities should be designed so that it may be divided into short-range and long-range undertakings, relating to priorities. One of the most important principles of good planning is that of setting priorities and sticking to them, assuming that the priorities genuinely do reflect the needs assessed.

In selecting activities, planners and developers must be aware of all impinging limits and constraints. A realistic analysis of what there is to work with and, equally important, what there is to work against must be readily at hand. It is essential to specify the limitations of time, money, program requirements, people, and facilities within which the program must operate. Also, the ground rules under which the program must function must be considered. Types of constraints might be identified with the following questions:

Social. Look at the total college and the community. Do the staff members accept the notion of staff development? Remember, in order to be effective, all groups involved must accept and participate in the various staff development activities. If they don't, the staff development program will fail.

Technological. What technological support will the staff development program have available? The program requires the use of materials, equipment, and facilities. Without these, the program cannot be successful. The use of a computer will greatly aid in the analysis of assessment and evaluation data.

Administrative. How is the staff development program to be coordinated, managed, and supervised? To whom does the staff report? What authority rests within the staff development program?

Political. What governance limits are placed upon the program? How political must the staff development staff be in order to survive? Is there adequate support within the governmental structure for this program from both college administrative staff and governing bodies?

Legal. Are there any laws or regulations which restrict or encourage staff development activities? Are there state certification or licensing requirements placed upon staff which can be fulfilled through staff development experiences? Should there be official documents, carrying board approval, prepared which outline the policies, procedures, and requirements of this program?

Economic. What kind of financial backing and commitment have been made? What are the sources of funding? What are the fiscal constraints placed upon the expenditure of funds?

Additional factors which affect program development are outside interest groups, professional associations, college/university personnel and programs, accrediting associations, students, and the educational community itself. Only by the examination of all these areas and the formulation of a comprehensive staff development plan will the college be able to move toward accomplishing the established goals and objectives of this program.

The Staff Development Plan should include the following information. The structure will reflect the needs of the specific community college, but a basic outline is:

A. Statement of philosophy
    1. General philosophy of the community college
    2. Philosophy of the staff development program
B. Needs assessment
C. Goals of the staff development program
D. Objectives for the staff development program
E. Action plan and activities
F. Calendar
G. Evaluation
H. Policies and procedures
I. Dissemination of activities and outcomes

Planning is a continuous cycle and requires at least annual revision. Constant monitoring is required. The planning document provides a structure and guide for operation. With it, conducting staff development activities is much easier; without it, the program is destined to fail. (See

Appendix B for Staff Development Planning Guide and Appendix C for a Checklist of Staff Development Planning Activities.)

CONDUCTING THE PROGRAM

The activities which comprise the staff development program are developed from the information collected in the planning process. The format of each activity will depend upon its purpose, audience, available resources, relationship to other college programs, and the creativity of the staff involved in planning and conducting each activity. The format will also be reflective of past activities and expectations of the college administration.

One of the first responsibilities in conducting the staff development activity is to establish a climate for learning. A climate conducive to learning requires comfortable physical surroundings—attractive decor, good ventilation, lighting, and arrangement of the room. But more than this is needed, for both the environment and the learner must be prepared before the message is delivered. If the environment presents too many obstacles, or if the learner is not ready, physically or emotionally, the perceptual process will falter. All of our mental processes depend upon our perception. Inadequate perceiving results in poor thinking, inappropriate responses and diminished interest in the topic at hand.

The success of any staff development activity depends upon the skills and abilities of the presenter. The presenter will be looked upon as the authority and so must display confidence in his/her role. In taking the leadership role, the presenter must utilize human relations skills as well as content expertise. These human relations skills are demonstrated in terms of the qualities of empathy, flexibility, ability to communicate (both verbally and nonverbally), objectivity, and fairness; expertise in problem solving, sensitivity, timing, and trouble-shooting; and skill in group dynamics. The presenter in inservice activities should be considered both an expert and a colleague, and be respected both as a professional person and as a human being. As "expert," the presenter will provide leadership and answers, solve problems, analyze and diagnose situations, and help participants find answers on their own. As "colleague," the presenter will be viewed as one of the group, knowing what the participants are experiencing because of having once sat in their places. The presenter can speak their language and relate to their situations because of having worked within the field. It is challenging and rewarding to balance the two roles successfully. The following suggestions are based on *Tips To Presenters* (11:62).

1. State clearly the desired outcomes.

2. Vary the techniques and activities.

3. Relate the objectives to each session.

4. Clarify the relationship of each session to the total program and the learning applicability.

5. Establish an open relationship seeking involvement and commitment.

6. Stress the advantages and usefulness of the learning taking place.

7. Emphasize the dimensions of the program — the aims, time schedule, tasks involved, etc.

8. Delineate the relationships between process and application, making it relevant and increasing the transfer of skills from inservice to the job.

9. Work within the established system constantly emphasizing support.

10. Develop leadership abilities in the participants so progress will continue.

11. Stress the value of feedback and evaluation as elements of growth.

12. Keep an open line of communication to continue after the inservice session.

13. Be confident in your expertise, relying on standards and guidelines of the profession.

14. Plan. Be organized. Communicate.

Planners and staff development program designers must carefully weigh the pros and cons of selecting someone from within or outside their community college. Presenters from within have the advantage of knowledge of the college and how it operates, the make-up of the faculty, the composition of the student body, and learning resources which are readily available. Someone from the outside, on the other hand, will not be involved in power plays or other counter-productive situations involving insiders. Frequently, because they are not part of the system, outsiders can be more objective and open in presenting the material, whereas insiders, though they may be the leading experts in the field, are frequently viewed with jealousy and as prophets without honor in their own land. An outsider may not experience this but may often not be accepted readily because participants feel that no one from outside can understand the particularities of "X" community college. The planned duration of an activity and the availability of outside presenters will also help in determining staff development staffing patterns and practices.

Regardless of the quality of the available outside cadre of experts, the college needs to develop its own internal group of persons who can conduct the various staff development activities. The occasional external consultant will provide a positive stimulus, but there is no replacement for a well developed, internally based staff development program.

Through interpersonal relationships and content skills, the presenter establishes effective instructional/learning relationships with the participants. The objective is to attempt to change behaviors, for behavior is the only thing that *can* be changed through the staff development process. Staff developers are attempting only to manage the behavior of the participants within institutional parameters; far too much conditioning has taken place for attitudes to be readily amenable to change. Work proceeds with each participant in terms of his needs in relation to the improved fulfillment of his job responsibilities.

From the very beginning, the presenter must endeavor to achieve a feeling of group unity and rapport. Each participant should begin to feel as a part of the group and become a contributor to accomplish the purposes of the activity. The presenter has the responsibility to keep the discussion moving, facilitate and promote ideas, moderate conflict, prevent domination by any one individual or group, steer the group toward closure, and aid in summarizing the activities. The size of the group will affect the presenter's role, for the larger the group the more "talk to" the presentation style frequently becomes. This is, however, a temptation to be resisted. The creative presenter will try to use a variety of presentation styles and resources which will assist in keeping learning lively and moving for all participants.

EVALUATING THE PROGRAM

As stated in the opening pages of this chapter, a staff de-

FORMATS
FOR
INSERVICE SESSIONS
(11:50)

PRESENTATIONS

LECTURE   DEMONSTRATION
PANEL   DEBATE
SKIT   ROLE PLAY
INTERVIEW   SIMULATION

GROUP ACTIVITIES

DISCUSSION   GAMES
ROLE PLAY   MINI-SESSIONS
SIMULATION   BRAINSTORMING
LABORATORY   CASE STUDY
CLINIC   FIELD ACTIVITY

INDIVIDUAL ACTIVITIES

SELF-INSTRUCTION   CASSETTES
PROGRAMMED INSTRUCTION   CONTRACT LEARNING
VIDEO-TAPES   LABORATORY
PRACTICE EXERCISE   IN-BASKET ACTIVITY
ACTION MAZE   DRILL

AUDIOVISUAL PRESENTATIONS

VIDEO-TAPE   TELEVISION
8MM CASSETTE   TRANSPARENCIES
SLIDE-TAPE   FLOW CHARTS
SOUND FILMSTRIPS   EXHIBITIONS
16MM FILMS

FIGURE 3

velopment program is a comprehensive plan of interrelated activities which enhance and further personal, instructional, and institutional needs. Staff development activities assist in accomplishing one of the major goals of the community college — the improvement of learning opportunities.

Because of its comprehensiveness and intrinsic nature, the evaluation of the staff development program is extremely complex. Activities take many forms, varying in scope and purpose. However, there are always common elements and these provide a basis upon which an evaluation plan can be developed and conducted. Evaluation should never be done in isolation or just for its own sake; its main purpose is to provide feedback to the staff so that performance can be improved. Evaluation is the only means for finding assistance and direction in redesigning existing programs or designing entirely new activities. It should be seen as an instrument intended to help the staff make better decisions.

The evaluation phase of the staff development program should be cooperatively developed with and supported by the college's overall evaluation staff. This collaboration and involvement will also insure the inclusion of this program in the college's total evaluation plan.

There are five basic questions which should serve as a preamble to the evaluation of staff development activities: (1) Why evaluate the activity? (2) What were we trying to do? (3) What shall we do in order to improve our activities? (4) How will we know we are making a success? and (5) How can we take advantage of and incorporate the information provided through the collection of data?

All staff development activities need to employ two kinds of evaluation. The first of these is *program* evaluation which provides insights into the activities in progress so that immediate and continuous adjustments can be made throughout the activity. Program evaluation is most effectively derived from ongoing participant reaction, discussion, questioning, and nonverbal communication and response to events occurring during the staff development activity. The second is *outcome* or *product* evaluation. This type of evaluation measures the degree to which the objectives were met — what, in fact, the results were. Several examples of outcome evaluation forms are given in Appendix D. Each of these types of evaluation must be built into the overall staff development plan from the beginning of the planning process in order to determine what information will be needed, how to acquire it, and how to use the data collected.

Before undertaking the design of an evaluation program, one must determine why the evaluation is to be done. Evaluation results can be used in many different ways. Is the data to be used to justify the present program of staff development activities? Is it to assist in making the staff development program accountable? Is it to assist in the management and improvement of staff development activities? Is it to help college administrators decide on matters relating to personnel management? According to how it is going to be used, the data needed will differ; therefore, the first step in planning for evaluation must be to determine what the purpose of the evaluation is to be. Only through preplanning can this be accomplished.

The mere collection of data is of little value. The results of evaluation need to be analyzed and organized according to the predetermined need. The data should be tabulated, with reports prepared and disseminated to all persons needing the information. It should always be evident that a major reason for evaluation is to assist people in making better decisions in the future. The positive, forward-looking aspects of the evaluation should far outweigh any others.

Just as staff development activities are to be nonthreatening, so must the evaluation process. Participants must be able to respond to the evaluation instrument honestly without fear of any repercussion. However, the data collected should also enable the staff development staff to conduct follow-up activities. Since the focus of staff development activities is change in behavior, follow-up activities need to be conducted which measure the degree to which the learned skill has become part of the participant's job performance. Thus the program comes full circle in relating to the fulfillment of personal, instructional, and institutional needs, goals, and objectives.

It is safe to say that no process will ever completely meet everyone's needs. For this reason, this chapter is to be considered as presenting only the beginnings. Staff development programs require much tailoring and development, in order to meet the community college's special needs. A wide range of persons should be involved in planning, conducting, and evaluating staff development activities. In summary, there are several points which need to be kept in the forefront of all staff development activities:

1. The activity must grow out of a need by and for the participants to know in a particular area;

2. Concerned persons must be involved in planning the activity;

3. Goals and objectives must be clearly stated and kept in mind;

4. Experiences must be provided for participants to share and learn together;

5. Necessary and adequate resources (personnel, materials, facilities, budget, time and program) must be made available;

6. Activities must start where the participants are and

proceed according to each individual's needs;

7. A continuous evaluation plan must be instituted which measures progress and assesses present and future directions.

A listing of staff development offerings compiled by the League for Innovation in the Community College can be found in Appendix E.

The leadership of the staff development program must be aware of the variety of skills and competencies needed by the staff in order for them to do their jobs more professionally. The leadership must be open to cooperative and coordinated endeavors. The responsible program staff must possess critical, motivational, leadership, organizational, and communicative skills. The staff development program cannot risk becoming static; it must constantly provide new opportunities for improvement, or it will decay and become nonfunctional, a program in name only. The staff development program will gain strength and stature if it is perceived by the college community as being strong, supportive, positive and helpful. It will quickly go downhill if it is preceived as fatuous, divisive, or a waste of time. Those programs that "have it" gain more; those that don't may be hopelessly "plowed under."

Chapter IV
Related Studies, Research and Development

Comprehensive surveys of community college learning resources programs have been conducted in a number of states, and several studies have been nationwide in scope. The majority of these studies have been aimed at describing specific programs or discussing standards and guidelines in relation to program development. This chapter will provide a focus upon a sampling of the pertinent studies and projects effecting the growth of the community college learning resources program. A veritable flurry of studies appeared in the early seventies, but fewer have been done since the mid-seventies. Thus, although a number of the studies cited were conducted nearly ten years ago, their findings are still relevant to the current and future development of learning resources programs.

A survey conducted by Pamela Reeves has provided considerable insight into learning resources centers. Through the use of a questionnaire mailed to 600 community colleges and a response from 250 of them, 53 colleges were selected for site visits. In addition to the basic institutional data collected, the author requested information about five aspects of the program of the learning resource center: (1) instruction in library use, (2) relations with the outside community, (3) collection-building, (4) staffing and public service, and (5) uses of automation. The investigation disclosed notable trends including strong audiovisual services, liberal circulation policies, and limited professional coverage. The services provided by the staff of the centers revealed a mixture of those services offered by a public library and a university library. (29)

In the summer 1972, Max R. Raines conducted a survey to determine the extent of community services and other related programs provided by learning resources centers. This survey was done in cooperation with the American Association of Junior Colleges (which had not as yet added "Community" to its name). Questionnaires were sent to colleges nominated by the membership of the AAJC as having outstanding programs. Those two-year institutions which received three or more nominations were automatically included in the study. Fifty-three programs were sent the questionnaire, and responses from forty colleges were included in the final report. One significant conclusion drawn from this study was that the degree of commitment by the colleges to community involvement was generally limited at that time. Although there was a growing awareness of the need for community services, the responses received did not warrant the conclusion that an immediate increase in services could be expected. The second part of the study identified current services which might provide prototypes for other institutions to adapt and adopt. (28)

In addition to the nationwide surveys which are available, a number of states have conducted studies regarding various aspects of learning resources center development. A noncomparative survey of the status of the development of educational media in Iowa's Area Community Colleges and Vocational Schools was conducted in 1972. Specific activities included on-campus visits, self-evaluation of the media programs in relationship to established criteria, inventory of resources and services, and local narrative descriptions of the media programs. (20)

The October 1970 issue of the *Kentucky Library Association Bulletin* reports a survey of Kentucky's community college learning resources centers. A questionnaire was mailed to the twenty-two Kentucky junior and community college libraries. The questionnaire collected data in the following areas: (1) general information, (2) finances, (3) physical stock collections, (4) circulation, (5) technical processes, and (6) buildings and equipment. The data collected documents the fact, even with this limited amount of information, that Kentucky's community colleges appeared to be experiencing the growth which was typical nationwide. (12)

A study on multimedia services in community colleges was completed in 1970 by the Survey Committee of the Illinois Library Association. In their study of the existing and planned roles of the community college learning resources centers in meeting educational needs of the total institution it is designed to serve, the committee included these categories: (1) philosophy, (2) staff, (3) budget, (4) collection, (5) facilities, (6) systems, and (7) services. The report contained specific recommendations that "if implemented would enhance the development of the total learning resources program of the community colleges of this state". (17)

A number of studies have been conducted regarding single institutional learning resources programs, and reference has been made throughout this book to various studies, reports, and articles which highlight one community college. Only one of these is cited here—a survey of the El Camino College Library, in Torrance, California.

The purpose of the El Camino College survey was to evaluate the relationship of the library and the instructional program. The data collection techniques included committee observations, interviews, and questionnaire responses from students, faculty, administrators, and members of the library staff. The committee concluded from its investigation that all groups surveyed, although aware of the roles of the library, did not make extensive demands of the library in their courses. There was a general lack of the initiative and leadership on the part of the faculty and the administration that is required to develop the library as an integral part of the instructional program. A major recommendation of the committee was to establish the administration and operation of the library and audiovisual services under the directorship of a Dean of Instructional Resources. A final conclusion was that the program would be costly but that the costs could be justified on the basis of improved instruction and student learning opportunities. (16)

During the fall semester of the 1969–1970 academic school year, Kenneth Allen (1) investigated the use of library programs in three community colleges in Illinois. Through the use of questionnaires to faculty, student, and those who entered the library, the data for the study were collected. A total of 1,312 questionnaires was administered.

The following are the findings from Allen's study. Since Allen administered three separate questionnaires, the findings are grouped accordingly.

A. Student questionnaire:

1. Seventy-four percent indicated that utilization of the library was necessary for academic success.

2. Seventy-two percent indicated the resources of the library met their needs.

3. Fifty percent responded that utilization of the library affected their final grade.

4. Seventy-two percent responded that they used other libraries in the community in addition to those of the colleges.

5. Thirty percent responded that they entered the library daily; forty-six percent weekly; sixteen percent month-

ly; and eight percent never entered the facility.

6. Fifty-one percent listed as their major reason for coming to the library study without using library materials; thirty-five percent to use library materials; eight percent to check out materials; four percent to use audiovisual materials for independent study; and three percent to find a friend.

7. Thirty-two percent had made the most use of the library for the social studies division; twenty-six percent for humanities; twenty-two percent for occupational; seventeen percent for mathematics and science; and three percent for physical education.

8. Sixty percent indicated they had consulted the librarian for assistance at some time.

B. Faculty questionnaire:

1. Seventy-one percent indicated their teaching techniques were affected because of a lack of library materials.

2. Sixty-two percent indicated they required their students to use the library.

3. Forty-five percent indicated they currently had books or audiovisual materials on reserve in the library.

C. "Door check" questionnaire

1. Sixty-one percent stated that their primary reason for coming to the library was to study; twenty-two percent came to use library materials; nine percent came to find a friend; five percent to

check out materials; and three percent to use audiovisual materials for independent study.

2. Eighty-nine percent accomplished their intended purpose.

3. Sixteen percent consulted the librarian.

4. Forty-four percent responded they were not using the library for a particular course; fifteen percent for social studies; fourteen percent for humanities; thirteen percent for mathematics and science; thirteen percent for occupational resources; and one percent for physical education (1:69-71)

From these findings a general community college user profile can be produced—a full-time, female student engaged in academic course work, enrolled in courses taught by faculty members with varying degrees of educational development, living with parents, receiving satisfactory grades, and coming from a higher socioeconomic background than the average student.

The following recommendations from Allen's study provide direction for the development of learning resources programs which would become important centers for learning.

1. The evidence within this investigation indicated that more attention should be devoted to meeting the library needs of all students enrolled in the various curricula, including those enrolled on a part-time and unclassified basis. The nature of the community colleges is such that they offer programs in the transfer, occupational, general studies, and continuing education curricula. This investigation reveals that the part-time and unclassified students made little use of the

library facility.

2. An increase in study facilities should be provided for the community college student in locations other than those of the library. A large percentage of students indicated they come to the library to study their own materials. The provision of study lounges outside the library would enable the student to find available study space closer to classes and at the same time free the library for students desiring to use library materials.

3. Students should be more than just "encouraged" to use library facilities, for, as shown by other studies, encouragement only does not increase utilization. The utilization patterns were lower than the attitudes of the faculty and students reflected. Perhaps faculty should give additional attention to developing courses for instruction centered around the library instead of depending on textbooks.

4. Size of the collection is not paramount in determining the effectiveness or quality of the library. Factors as important as size include the following: size of the institution, the geographical location, the attitudes of the students and the faculty, and the age of the institution. Evaluation teams for accreditation should remember that the success of the library is a more adequate measure than the size of the collection. (1:74–75)

Three studies report findings which have implications still for the development of the community college instructional program. In 1962, Kelley (19) conducted a study of the practices in the area of supervision of curriculum and instruction in California public community colleges. He recommended that a comprehensive study be made of the criteria needed for directing junior college instruction. The burden of responsibility for improving the curricula was largely that of the deans or directors of instruction, who had only recently been added to the organizational structure, and these officials were in great need of a set of criteria with which to measure the process and success of their roles. A study was designed to establish these criteria. (19:6)

Howard Crouch (5) investigated criteria which could be used in the construction of community college curricula. It was found that whatever criteria are established, the curriculum should provide the student the opportunity to study, discuss, and understand interests, aptitudes, and abilities in relation to appropriate job opportunities. (5:206) The purposes of Crouch's study were (1) to investigate bio-socio-psychological characteristics of post-adolescent problems, (2) to derive criteria implied by these problems which could guide curricular construction, (3) to discover to what degree authorities in the field believe such criteria to be of major importance, (4) to determine the extend to which existing curricula meet these criteria, and (5) to recommend standards to community college curriculum makers. (5:1)

Keuscher (21) studied ten Southern California community colleges in order to collect data which would enable him to provide indicators as to what type of organizational climate is needed if the college administration desires to have an innovative school. He found that administrators who expect added resources, new facilities, technological gadgetry, or organizational panaceas to bring about the desired result may be disappointed. The characteristics of openness are more important in fostering innovation than any other single factor or component.

One research study was concerned with community college library practices. Helen Wheeler (31) describes and identifies ways in which the community college library program can be and should be meeting the needs of the institution of which it is a part. Through a questionnaire and on-site visits, Wheeler concluded that—

1. the way in which the library can best serve the unique needs and functions of a community college program at present is an overall improvement both quantitative and qualitative, to provide minimal basic library service, with attention most urgently needed in the areas of staffing, collection, and seating; and,

2. many community college libraries are unable to serve their institutions effectively because of lack of funds, although,

3. knowledge of techniques of professional library service and of the unique functions of the community college is possessed by the library directors as evidenced by their backgrounds, reports, or practices and goals. (30:2)

Sparked by the need for sharing information and resources and by the realization that innovative practices require a team approach for development and dissemination, the League for Innnovation in the Community College was founded in 1968. The League is the oldest community college consortium in the United States. In 1979 its membership consisted of seventeen community college districts which included fifty-two public institutions and more than one-half million students in twelve states. The League, a voluntary national consortium, continues to project its original goal of stimulating innovation and experimentation. The League for Innovation is also dedicated to evaluation in all areas of community college development.

Specifically, the League seeks to accomplish its purposes by assisting its members to:

1. experiment in teaching, learning, student services, and other aspects of community college operation;

2. share results of experiments;

3. share conceptual planning and learning objectives;

4. exchange instructional materials and procedures designed to enhance learning;

5. examine the relevance of varied modes of college administration to experimentation in teaching and learning;

6. provide a common base for research on the effects of varied innovative practices by gathering and sharing data on students, programs, and modes of organization; and

7. evaluate the impact of the institution's practices on its students and its community.

Robert Leo, of the League staff, says that the League is able to continue to influence community college development throughout the nation because its membership can be found in all sections of the country. The League is not only committed to programs that contribute to the continuing improvement of member colleges; it also provides opportunities for other community colleges to participate in its workshops, conferences, projects, and activities. Among the League's activities have been such projects as—

1. an institute for implementing a systems approach to instruction within community colleges with high minority enrollment;

2. a project for training community college personnel in educational management;

3. international projects in Egypt, India, Africa, Yugo-
slavia, Mexico, and Jordan;

4. a project on implementing instructional development
through learning resources centers;

5. a project for training faculty in solar energy systems;

6. a project for training faculty in household/personal
financial planning;

7. a Project Usher on educational management;

8. a health instruction exchange;

9. a workshop on a systems approach to teaching biology;

10. summer conferences for division chairpersons; and

11. an institute to articulate new developments in the
teaching of college physics.

During the past decade the League has emerged as a
major force contributing to the growth and development of
community colleges through a program of systematically
designed projects, conferences, and publications. It has held
over thirty-one conferences and workshops and sponsored
nearly thirty externally funded projects at a funding level of
more than $2,250,000. In short, the League is viable, well,
and the prognosis for the future is most healthy.

The League operates under the direction of a seventeen-
member board of directors comprised of the chief administrator of each member district. Its office is staffed by an
executive director, an associate executive director, a coordinator of special projects, and two secretaries. A League

representative is designated in each of the seventeen
member districts to initiate and coordinate League activities. League activities are funded by membership dues,
foundation grants, government contracts, and income from
publications, conferences, and workshops. Membership in
the League is by invitation; the current policy of the board
is to admit no more than seventeen members.

In the mid-seventies, five community colleges organized a
nonprofit corporation, the Association of Community Colleges for Excellence in Systems and Services (ACCESS) with
the goal of making learning available to as many people as
possible and at times and places most convenient for them.
In order to accomplish this, it was necessary to design
resources that different colleges could use, both flexibly and
economically, to serve a growing *adult* student body.
Member colleges organized faculty teams to develop, in
conjunction with two commercial companies, high quality
resources that would satisfy a wide range of educational
needs. The result was a print and video program designed to
be used in a wide variety of instructional settings—in the
community college classroom, over closed circuit television,
on open circuit or cable television, and in a rapid transmission and storage system. Chicago's Magna Systems is leading
the way in an exciting use of video discs for education. Their
courses in adult education, complete with study guides, are
already a part of the curriculum for ACCESS.

With this flexibility, the four programs developed (each
consisting of thirty half-hour videotapes and text) can be
used as a part of the general education program or in
conjunction with any adult education program. The four
programs were entitled *Consumer Education*, *Child
Development*, *Introduction to Business*, and *Your Health,
Your Choice*.

What makes this program unique is its RTS (Rapid
Transmission and Storage) distribution system. This system
was developed by the late Peter C. Goldmark of the

Goldmark Communications Corporation, in Stamford, Connecticut. The system can store up to thirty hours of video programming on a single, standard, one-hour video tape. As many as thirty different programs can be viewed simultaneously from one tape, which means that thirty different classrooms or individuals could be receiving video programming simultaneously from one tape. The programs can be broadcast in real time over any medium over which a television signal can be sent, such as broadcast television, cable, microwave, or satellite. The programs can also be transmitted at thirty times normal speed over the same media. Thus distribution time is more rapid and less costly than with other systems. Still on the threshold of emerging into wider use, however, it is a development to watch for since it has numerous implications for learning resources programs and instructional activities.

In 1977, the American Association of Community and Junior Colleges and a group of its member institutions who were involved in the production and use of high-quality television courses established an office in Washington, D.C. Through the efforts of this office, the Task Force on the Uses of Mass Media for Learning was formed. According to James Zigerall, Director of the Office of Mass Media Learning, the Task Force's major goals are (1) encouraging and assisting more community colleges in the use of television and media-based courses, (2) encouraging greater cooperation and exchange of information and materials among television course designers and users, and (3) helping to frame AACJC policy and positions on issues that affect the uses of mass media in education.

Thus far the Task Force has issued two major publications. One, the *Mass Media Catalog*, is a descriptive compilation of approximately one hundred quality courses now available for use. The second, titled *Using Mass Media for Learning*, is a collection of articles on using the mass media in post-secondary education.

Task Force members are coordinating their course production planning, collaborating on production projects, and identifying common media-based curriculum needs. They are also making their views and recommendations known to representatives of governmental agencies that are drawing up telecommunications policies which will affect instructional broadcasters in years to come.

The Task Force staff are available to provide assistance to community colleges interested in using television and other media in their programs of instruction. The office also maintains an up-to-date collection of samples of mass media courses and associated study materials that AACJC members are invited to consult.

Membership in the Task Force includes: Bergen Community College, New Jersey; City Colleges of Chicago; Coast Community College District, California; Dallas Community College District; Milwaukee Area Technical College; Miami-Dade Community College; Northern Virginia Community College; and the Southern California Consortium for Community College TV. Several of the members have earned national reputations as producers and distributors of television courses. All are making extensive use of TV and media-based courses an important part of their services. Due to the growing interest in media-based instruction throughout the community college field, the impact of the Task Force has been effective and influential.

Mediated instruction is coming of age in the community colleges. Faculty members are designing and producing, in cooperation with instructional design specialists, instructional packages which better meet the needs of students. The literature stresses the concept of incorporating all resources (print, nonprint, and the equipment for proper use) into one agency. The program of service must be developed around the needs of each individual community college's goals and objectives.

Based on the literature and the other activities cited, the

author concludes that if innovation is to become a key element and widely accepted in program development, then the administration, the faculty, the learning resources staff, the students, and the community must be dedicated to exploring alternative teaching and learning methods. Without the support of all persons involved, the program cannot succeed.

With the continuing importance of the relationship between the community college and the community, it can be expected that future studies and projects will focus upon the benefits which can be derived from a cooperatively developed partnership. Community colleges will be changing their organizational patterns, methods of delivering their instructional programs, course offerings, and resource needs. Already, cooperative projects are emerging which involve other educational institutions, information agencies, governmental bodies, business/industrial organizations, and volunteer groups. These cooperative ventures are being planned for and actively developed; they don't just happen. This cooperation enables the community college to reinforce and supplement rather than duplicate available community services and to bring new dimension and scope to the role of the community colleges.

Chapter V
Report of Questionnaire Findings

OVERVIEW

The findings in this portion of the book are based upon the responses received in 150 usable questionnaires (see Appendix F) from the 175 questionnaires returned by the directors of learning resources programs across the country. These 150 responses represented 47 percent of the total number of questionnaires mailed.

Selecting one of the following descriptions, the respondents were asked to identify the organizational and administrative title of their own learning resources facility. The *number* to the left indicates the number of those selecting that description; the *percent* is the percentage of the total 150 colleges selecting that description.

No.	Percentage	
98	65	*Learning Resources Center (LRC).* A unit organized to provide a full range of instructionally related print and nonprint services encompassing instructional design and development services administered as a single program under the leadership of one director.
24	16	*Media Center (MC).* A unit organized to provide a full range of print and

nonprint materials, necessary equipment, and services from the media staff to fulfill user requests.

10   7   *Central Library (CL)*. A unit geared primarily to provide information in a print format, organized, stored, and retrieved to fulfill user requests.

3   2   *Audiovisual Center (AVC)*. A unit organized to provide primarily nonprint services and the necessary equipment for proper utilization and distributed upon user request.

8   5   *Central Library–Audiovisual Center (CL—AVC)*. Eight community colleges had separate Central Libraries and Audiovisual Centers, but elected to respond jointly to the above two titles. A separate category was added to reflect these responses.

0   0   *Classroom Library*. An area maintained in the instructional rooms where materials are shelved without benefit of centralized organization.

0   0   *Office Library*. An area maintained in the individual areas provided faculty members where materials are shelved without benefit of centralized organization.

7   5   Other

The seven colleges checking the "other" category of facilities included the following: three with tutorial/skills laboratory centers; two having a media center and central library; one with a learning resource center, except for books and microfilm, and a separate central library containing microfilm; and one with an instructional resource center and a separate library.

The average enrollment of the 150 community colleges was 3,124 full-time students and 4,248 part-time students. For each facility type, the greatest number of responses was in the category of 3001 or more students.

The average number of faculty members employed in the community colleges was 143 full-time and 134 part-time. For each facility type, the greatest number of responses was in the category of 151 or more faculty members.

More than 92 percent of the colleges were housed on permanent, separate campuses, while 47 percent were located in suburban areas.

Sixty-five percent of the responses identified the organization and administration of the learning resources facility as being a learning resources center. Sixteen percent of the colleges indicated that they had media centers. Therefore, learning resources were administered as one unit in 74 percent of the colleges.

In almost half of the colleges, the percentage of the total college budget allocated to learning resources for all purposes ranged between 4 and 7. The average percentage allocated to purchase learning resources was 5.5.

The average square footage occupied by learning resources centers was 28,107 square feet. More than 45 percent of the colleges responded that 24,000 or more square feet had been allocated to the learning resources program. In more than 60 percent of the colleges, the total space assigned to the learning resources program was in one building.

Of the colleges responding, almost 95 percent indicated that their learning resources were available during class hours, while 67 percent indicated that the resources were available for evening and weekend use during times classes were not being held. These resources were available during vacation and holiday periods in more than 60 percent of the colleges.

The average number of paid professional personnel working in the learning resources program was six full-time and two part-time persons. Of the colleges responding, 38 percent had between four and six full-time professionals, and almost half of the colleges had no part-time paid professional persons. More than half of the professional staff worked a twelve-month contract.

In 92 percent of the colleges, the learning resources staff had faculty rank and status. The responses indicated an average of five professional staff in each of the 130 colleges granting faculty rank and status to the learning resources professional personnel. In 70 percent of the responses, it was indicated that key learning resources personnel were not assigned additional responsibilities unrelated to the operation of the learning resources program.

The most frequently mentioned title of the principal learning resources staff member responsible for the program was that of director. This principal staff member reported to an academic dean in almost 60 percent of the colleges. These persons worked under a twelve-month contract in three-fourths of the community colleges. In more than 88 percent of the responses, the principal learning resources staff member was responsible for the development of the learning resources program's annual budget.

The number of paid support personnel, not including professional staff, varied. Of the colleges responding, approximately eight of every ten did not employ full-time aides, students, or any other type of full-time support personnel. Over 70 percent of the colleges did employ full-time clerks, with an average of five clerks per college. Two-thirds of the colleges employed full-time technicians, with an average of four each.

The number of colleges not employing part-time paid support personnel, such as aides, clerks, or technicians, was more than 75 percent in each instance. However, 67 percent of the colleges did employ part-time student help, averaging seventeen part-time students each.

In over 60 percent of the colleges, professional staff members in the learning resources program were assigned on a part-time basis to work on instructional development activities with faculty members. Only 22 percent of the colleges reported that professional staff worked full time on instructional development activities. Thirty percent of the colleges reported that non-professional staff were assigned part time, and twelve percent that they were assigned full time to instructional development work with faculty members.

Materials were grouped by format and filed on open shelves in three-fourths of the colleges, and almost 20 percent indicated that materials, regardless of format, were interfiled on open shelves. All materials were made easily accessible in nearly all the colleges, restrictions being made on such things as special collections or rare items. Equipment to use these materials was available for use within the learning resources areas and classrooms. Almost 94 percent of the colleges provided preview of materials for faculty members. Interlibrary loans were reported as being arranged for faculty in over 98 percent of the colleges and for students in over 84 percent of the colleges.

The most popular forms of informing community college personnel of learning resources programs and materials were through bibliographies (82 percent), orientation sessions (75 percent), and displays (68 percent). The administration was informed of the needs of the learning resources program through reports and office meetings.

The most often given reason for reevaluation of the collection by the staff was the purchase of newer materials available (97 percent) and changing curriculum content (90 percent).

Two-thirds of the colleges had a faculty handbook available, and over 70 percent a student handbook which fully described all facets of the learning resources program. Policy statements governing the operation of the program were readily available for use by faculty, students, and administrators in 71 percent of the colleges.

The community college staff was informed of new acquisitions most frequently through bulletins (76 percent). In 85 percent of the colleges, the learning resources program served as a clearinghouse for all requests for new materials and in 78 percent, as a clearinghouse for all requests for new equipment. Of the colleges responding, 82 percent made a professional collection of materials available for faculty use.

In 60 percent of the colleges, the staff of the learning resources program participated as members of a teaching team. The staff of the learning resources program were involved most frequently in cooperative activities with other community groups and organizations through conferences (77 percent) and visits (77 percent). Three-fourths of the colleges indicated that learning resources staff served on curriculum committees. Nine out of every ten of the institutions reported that planning with faculty members helped to keep the staff of the learning resources program informed about future assignments and needs. The responses were nearly equal between "slight" and "moderate" learning resources staff involvement in planning curricula changes and teaching/learning innovations.

Of the twenty-two instructional services listed in the survey instrument, six were provided to faculty members by more than 90 percent of the community colleges, which reported generally "medium" usage. The most popular services included (1) ordering new print materials on request, (2) having audiodiscs or tape recordings available on request for individuals from specific classes, (3) having visual materials available on request for individual assignments for specific classes, (4) producing audio recordings in any format, (5) providing consultation on materials needed in special subject areas, and (6) providing instruction in the use of the learning resources program.

Five services provided to the faculty had a response of 80 to 89 percent and six other services offered had responses from 70 to 79 percent of the colleges. Therefore, 77 percent of the services offered were being provided by more than 70 percent of the colleges' learning resources programs.

The four services with the lowest number of responses from colleges offering the services to faculty members included (1) production of computer-assisted instruction programs, (2) observation of students in the center for purposes of sharing with faculty information about interests, needs, and habits of study and reading behavior, (3) provision of a program whereby instructional materials and methods could be evaluated according to their teaching effectiveness, and (4) provision of a listing of community resources which supported the college's instructional program.

The staff of the learning resources program, in nine out of every ten colleges, worked with faculty members to assist them in integrating instructional resources into their teaching. The most frequently used services reported were (1) assistance given to individual faculty members as well as departments and units (80 percent), (2) assistance given in the production and use of materials which were used outside the learning resources program facilities (62 percent), and (3) assistance provided faculty members in all phases of producing learning packages (56 percent).

Health careers, social studies, and science were the instructional areas in which the learning resources program had the greatest impact. Colleges considered the programs' greatest success in supporting or influencing instruction to be of two kinds: one, the cooperation between the learning resource staff and the teaching faculty; and the other, the full range of services being provided. Budget difficulties, faculty resistance to change, and insufficient staff were indicated as the major difficulties in supporting or influencing instruction by the learning resources program staff.

DOCUMENTATION

Responses to the questions are tallied, individually and as a total group, according to the six facility types. For convenience, the six facility types are referred to throughout the tables in this chapter by their initials.

Learning Resources Center	LRC
Media Center	MC
Central Library	CL
Audiovisual Center	AVC
Central Library–Audiovisual Center	CL–AVC
Classroom Library	eliminated
Office Library	eliminated
Other	Other

The responses for several items on the questionnaire are also tabulated according to their regional accrediting association. Regional accrediting associations and their corresponding states are;

New England Association of Colleges and Secondary Schools, Inc. (NE)
> Connecticut
> Maine
> Massachusetts
> New Hampshire
> Rhode Island
> Vermont

Middle States Association of Colleges and Secondary Schools (M)

> Delaware
> District of Columbia
> Maryland
> New Jersey
> New York

Pennsylvania

Southern Association of Colleges and Schools (S)

Alabama
Florida
Georgia
Kentucky
Louisiana
Mississippi
North Carolina
South Carolina
Tennessee
Texas
Virginia

North Central Association of Colleges and Secondary Schools (NC)

Arizona
Arkansas
Colorado
Illinois
Indiana
Iowa
Kansas
Michigan
Minnesota
Missouri
Nebraska
New Mexico
North Dakota
Ohio
Oklahoma
South Dakota
West Virginia

Wisconsin
Wyoming

Northwest Association of Secondary and Higher Schools (NW)

Alaska
Idaho
Montana
Nevada
Oregon
Utah
Washington

Western Association of Schools and Colleges (W)

California
Hawaii

Each of the six regional accrediting associations has played a role in the development of community college learning resources programs. Standards relating to the learning resources programs have been developed and are used during accreditation team visits. It is, therefore, appropriate to report several findings according to the six regions.

TABLE 1

Frequency Distribution of Regional
Response to Initial Questionnaires

Community Colleges	REGIONS						
	NE	M	S	NC	NW	W	Total
Number receiving questionnaire	11	71	85	74	19	62	322
Number responding	6	31	45	34	8	26	150
Percentage Responding	54	44	53	46	42	42	47

In most regions, the responses were proportionate to the number of community colleges receiving the questionnaire. For instance, the southern region represents 27 percent of the total population surveyed; 30 percent of the responses to the questionnaire are from the southern region.

TABLE 2

A FREQUENCY DISTRIBUTION OF FACILITY TYPES
IN COMMUNITY COLLEGES BY REGION

	REGIONS						
Facility Type	NE	M	S	NC	NW	W	Total
LRC	3	21	31	25	5	13	98
MC	3	2	8	4	3	4	24
CL	0	2	4	3	0	1	10
AVC	0	0	1	1	0	1	3
CL-AVC	0	5	0	1	0	2	8
Other	0	1	1	0	0	5	7
Total	6	31	45	34	8	26	150

Two out of every three community colleges responding indicated that they have a learning resource center facility. Among the regions, the highest facility type reported, (ranging from 50 to 74 percent) was the learning resources center. The western region had the greatest variety of facilities with six different types reported. The north central region reported that 74 percent of its community colleges had learning resources centers; this constituted the highest concentration of this facility type.

The remainder of this chapter is divided into five sections corresponding to the sections appearing in the questionnaire (Appendix F):

1. Community College Profile
2. Organization and Administration of Learning Resources
3. Arrangement and Accessibility of Learning Resources
4. Instructional Services

5. Instructional Development

Most responses are reported as percentages. In several questions, where the average figure and the range are significant, the data are so reported.

COMMUNITY COLLEGE PROFILE

Student Enrollment. The full-time enrollment of the 146 community colleges responding to this item ranged from 144 to 16,522. The number of part-time students range from 25 to 50,000 in the 133 responding community colleges.

TABLE 3

AVERAGE STUDENT ENROLLMENT
BY FACILITY TYPE

| Type of Enrollment | FACILITY TYPE | | | | | | |
	LRC	MC	CL	AVC	CL-AVC	Other	Total
Full-time	2,915	3,193	1,701	5,225	4,280	5,777	3,124
Part-time	3,899	4,755	1,877	10,338	6,146	7,072	4,248
Total	97	23	9	3	8	6	146

TABLE 4

FREQUENCY DISTRIBUTION OF
ENROLLMENT IN RELATION TO FACILITY TYPE

| | FACILITY TYPE | | | | | | | | | | | | |
| | LRC | | MC | | CL | | AVC | | CL-AVC | | OTHER | | TOTAL | |
Enrollment	FT	PT	FT	PT	FT	PT	FT	PT	FT	PT	FT	PT	FT	PT
1–1000	23	32	7	7	2	5	0	0	1	1	0	1	33	46
1001– 2000	31	14	5	5	4	2	0	0	0	1	0	0	40	22
2001– 3000	11	8	3	2	1	0	0	0	3	0	1	1	19	11
3001 +	32	34	8	6	2	3	3	2	4	5	5	4	54	54
Total	97	88	23	20	9	10	3	2	8	7	6	6	146	133

Colleges reporting an audiovisual center, a central library-audiovisual center, and other facility types had large full-time and part-time enrollments, mainly 2001 to 3000 full-time and 3001 or more part-time or above. On the other hand, the learning resources center, media center, and central library facility types enrollments were spread among all four enrollment categories. All part-time enrollment averages were higher than those for full-time enrollment.

TABLE 5

FREQUENCY DISTRIBUTION OF
FULL-TIME STUDENT ENROLLMENT BY REGION

| Enrollment | REGIONS | | | | | | |
	NE	M	S	NC	NW	W	Total
1–1000	1	11	12	9	0	0	33
1001–2000	4	6	16	6	2	6	40
2001–3000	1	5	5	4	2	2	19
3001 +	0	8	10	15	4	17	54
Total	6	30	43	34	8	25	146

Of the 146 responding community colleges, more than one-third (37 percent) had a full-time enrollment of more than 3000 students. A tabulation of the western region revealed that 68 percent of its colleges were in this 3001 or more category. The northwest and north central regions had 50 percent and 44 percent respectively, which represents the largest concentration of responses from these colleges in any of the population categories.

The New England and southern regions had the largest concentration of responses in the 1001 to 2000 category, while the middle region had the highest concentration of its responses (37 percent) in the 1 to 1000 category.

Only 13 percent of the colleges had full-time enrollments between 2001 and 3000. The only other region showing a distinguishing percentage was the New England region. Of the six responding schools, 67 percent were in the 1001 to

2000 category, while there were no responses in the 3001 or more category.

Faculty Members. The range of full-time faculty was from 13 to 1,245. The average for the 145 colleges was 143 faculty members.

TABLE 6

FREQUENCY DISTRIBUTION OF FACULTY MEMBERS IN RELATION TO FACILITY TYPE

Number of Faculty	LRC		MC		CL		AVC		CL-AVC		OTHER		TOTAL	
	FT	PT	FT	PT	FT	PT	FT	PT	FT	PT	FT	PT	FT	PT
1– 25	3	22	0	8	1	2	0	1	0	1	0	2	4	36
26– 50	14	15	3	2	1	2	0	1	0	1	0	0	18	21
51– 75	15	8	6	0	2	3	1	0	1	1	0	1	25	11
76–100	17	8	5	1	3	1	0	0	1	1	0	0	26	11
101–125	8	1	5	3	1	0	0	0	0	0	1	1	15	5
126–150	6	7	1	2	0	0	0	0	0	0	0	0	7	9
151 +	32	32	3	6	2	0	2	1	6	5	5	2	50	46
Total	95	93	23	22	10	8	3	3	8	8	6	6	145	140
Average	144	140	101	107	100	50	172	123	249	209	207	157	143	134

For the 140 colleges completing this question, the part-time faculty average was 134. In all community college facility types, with the exception of the media center, the average for part-time faculty was lower than for full-time. The responses ranged from 2 to 1,109.

The responses to the number of full-time and part-time faculty members are divided into categories of 25 each through 151 or more. The largest concentration of answers was in the category of 151 or more, with 35 percent for full-time faculty and 33 percent for part-time faculty. Four facility types had their highest concentration of full-time employed faculty members in the 151 or more category.

Campus Location. Of the 150 community colleges responding, 139 (93 percent) were on permanent, separate campuses. Six colleges were located on partially temporary campuses, while five were on completely temporary campuses. Campus location by facility type revealed the greatest concentration of each type on permanent separate campuses.

TABLE 7

FREQUENCY DISTRIBUTION OF COLLEGE LOCATION
IN RELATION TO FACILITY TYPE

Location	FACILITY TYPE						Total
	LRC	MC	CL	AVC	CL-AVC	Other	
Metropolitan	16	9	1	1	1	1	29
Suburban	46	8	4	2	7	4	71
Rural	31	6	5	0	0	2	44
Other	5	1	0	0	0	0	6
Total	98	24	10	3	8	7	150

Almost half (47 percent) of the community colleges reported that they were located in a suburban setting. The largest concentration by facility type also appeared in a suburban location. Other college locations reported were urban, small town/industrial, multi-campus, and outlying industrial/commercial zones.

ORGANIZATION AND ADMINISTRATION OF LEARNING RESOURCES

Organization. Learning resources on the campuses responding were administered as one unit in three out of every four instances. It should be noted that there was a distinct division between the responses of the learning resources centers and media centers and those of the four remaining facility types. The learning resources center and media center programs were generally administered as one unit, while the central library, audiovisual center, central library–audiovisual center, and others were administered almost exclusively as two or more units. Nearly 75 percent of all full-time students were enrolled in institutions where learning resources were administered as one unit.

TABLE 8

RELATIONSHIP OF ADMINISTRATIVE UNIT
TO FACILITY TYPE

			FACILITY TYPE				
Unit	LRC	MC	CL	AVC	CL-AVC	Other	Total
One	89	19	2	0	1	0	111
Two or more	9	5	8	3	7	7	39
Total	98	24	10	3	8	7	150

Budget. The pattern of allocating funds for learning resources was similar throughout the six regions. Seventy of the colleges allocated between 4 and 7 percent of the college's total budget to learning resources. This category (4 to 7 percent) included the highest percentage of responses in each region.

The 132 community colleges responding to this question averaged 5.5 percent of their total college budget for learning resources. The range for the learning resources center colleges was from 1 to 12 percent. The learning resources center colleges were slightly higher than the average since 5.6 percent of their budgets were allocated for learning resources.

More than half of the full-time students were enrolled in community colleges which allocated between 4 and 7 percent of their total budget for learning resources.

Space. The 128 colleges responding to this question reported that their facilities of various types occupied an average of 28,107 square feet. The learning resources center

TABLE 9

FREQUENCY DISTRIBUTION OF COLLEGE BUDGET
ALLOCATION BY FACILITY TYPE

Percentage of Budget	FACILITY TYPE						
	LRC	MC	CL	AVC	CL-AVC	Other	Total
Under 3%	16	5	1	1	5	3	31
4–7%	48	13	5	0	1	3	70
8–11%	24	3	0	0	1	0	28
12–15%	1	0	0	1	1	0	3
Total	89	21	6	2	8	6	132

had an average of 29,831 square feet, while the media center averaged 19,850 square feet. Central library colleges had the largest square footage, averaging 35,244 square feet. The smallest average of 3,945 square feet was found in audiovisual center colleges. The range was from 882 to 129,262 square feet.

Sixty-two percent of the community colleges reported that their learning resources were centralized. However, the central library, central library–audiovisual center, and others had the greatest percentage of answers in the decentralized category. The learning resources center, media center, and audiovisual center had a range of 66 percent to 78 percent of their facilities falling into the centralized category.

TABLE 10

FREQUENCY DISTRIBUTION OF LOCATION
OF LEARNING RESOURCES BY FACILITY TYPE

Location	FACILITY TYPE						
	LRC	MC	CL	AVC	CL-AVC	Other	Total
Centralized	65	18	3	2	2	2	92
Decentralized	33	5	7	1	6	5	57
Total	98	23	10	3	8	7	149

Accessibility to the Facility. Ninety-five percent of the 150 community colleges responded that their learning resources were available during class hours. There was more variety in responses concerning the availability of facilities during evening and weekend time when classes were not in session. One hundred and one community colleges (67 percent) stated that learning resources were available during evening and weekend hours.

Responses about availability during vacation and holiday periods varied. When queried about their availability, ninety-two community colleges (61 percent) said that their facilities are open during this time. Central libraries showed that 30 percent of their facilities were open, while the audiovisual centers and central library–audiovisual centers respond that their facilities were available at all times.

TABLE 11

AVERAGE NUMBER OF PROFESSIONAL PERSONNEL
EMPLOYED IN LEARNING RESOURCES PROGRAMS
BY FACILITY TYPE

Personnel	FACILITY TYPE						
	LRC	MC	CL	AVC	CL-AVC	Other	Total
Full-time	6.5	4.0	4.1	1.3	8.75	13.8	6.3
Part-time	2.14	2.0	7.5	0	3.0	3.5	2.38

Professional Personnel. The number of full time (FT) professional personnel employed in learning resources programs of the various types ranged from 1 to 45 persons. The average number of professional staff was 6.33. The largest concentration of responses (38 percent) were in the 4 to 6 category, while 33 percent of the responses were in the 1 to 3 category. Only two of the twelve colleges reporting 13 or more full-time professional staff were not in the learning resources center facility type.

In every facility type except the media center, 49 percent of responding community colleges did not employ any part-time (PT) professionals. In those community colleges having media centers, 60 percent employed between one and three part-time professionals. Totally, 42 percent of the colleges employed between one and three part-time professionals.

TABLE 12

NUMBER OF PROFESSIONAL PERSONNEL EMPLOYED IN
LEARNING RESOURCES IN RELATION TO TYPE OF FACILITY

No. of Personnel	LRC FT	LRC PT	MC FT	MC PT	CL FT	CL PT	AVC FT	AVC PT	CL-AVC FT	CL-AVC PT	OTHER FT	OTHER PT	TOTAL FT	TOTAL PT
0	0	45	0	7	0	7	0	3	0	5	0	3	0	70
1–3	28	41	12	12	5	1	3	0	0	2	0	3	48	59
4–6	38	7	9	0	3	0	0	0	3	1	2	0	55	8
7–9	14	2	1	1	0	0	0	0	1	0	2	0	18	3
10–12	6	0	1	0	1	1	0	0	4	0	1	1	13	2
13–15	5	0	0	0	0	0	0	0	0	0	1	0	6	0
16 +	5	0	0	0	0	0	0	0	0	0	1	0	6	0
Total	96	95	23	20	9	9	3	3	8	8	7	7	146	142

In reporting the number of professional staff by region, the western and southern regions' mode of responses were in the lowest grouping of one to three professional staff. In all other regions, the mode appeared in the four to six professional staff category.

It is revealed from the data that in the New England region, no college employed more than six staff members, and the northwest region had only two colleges with more than six staff members. The western region had 42 percent of its colleges with seven or more professional staff, including 11 percent (three colleges) with sixteen or more staff.

Seven out of every ten colleges reported between one and six full-time professional staff members, regardless of what percentage of the total budget was allocated for learning resources. Half of the colleges employing between one and three full-time staff allocated between 4 and 7 percent of their college budget to learning resources, while slightly more than half of the colleges employing four to six professional full-time staff allocated between 4 and 7 percent.

Those colleges employing one to three full-time learning resources staff more frequently had full-time enrollment figures of less than 2,000. While 50 percent of the colleges employing four to six full-time staff showed that their institutions enrolled fewer than 2,000 students, the other 50 percent enrolled more than 2,000 full-time students. Eighteen of the twenty-four colleges employing ten or more full-time professional staff enrolled more than 3,000 full-time students.

More than half (52 percent) of all the professional staff of the 148 community colleges responding to the question were employed under a twelve-month contract. Almost one-fourth (24 percent) were employed with a ten-month contract. More than 90 percent of the community colleges did extend faculty rank to the learning resource staff members. The number of staff having faculty rank ranged from 0 to 21 staff members; however, the greatest concentration of answers were found in the one through seven range (77 percent). Seventeen percent of the community colleges had three staff members with faculty rank, the highest response to any one figure. The average number of staff members having faculty rank per community college was 4.74.

In examining the data by the facility type, the figures closely resembled those of the 141 responding community colleges. More than 73 percent of the learning resources centers reported that between one and seven staff members had faculty rank.

Seven out of every ten learning resource personnel were not assigned additional responsibilities outside the program area. Those additional responsibilities that were assigned included teaching, membership on college and intercollegiate committees, grant procurement, advising students, and general administrative assignments.

Principal Learning Resources Staff Person. Director was the title used by more than 55 percent of the responding colleges to designate the principal staff member responsible for the learning resources program. Almost 17 percent of the colleges used the title librarian. The seven other titles, which have varying response rates, ranging from 1 to 8 percent, included chairperson, coordinator, dean, assistant dean, associate dean, other, and none.

In analyzing the titles by region, the responses were very similar to those for the total population. The western region showed the most diversity, with the use of nine different titles reported. Only 34 percent of the respondents used director to designate the principal learning resources staff member.

In the analysis of the titles as related to full-time student enrollment categories, the title director represented the greatest percentage of the responses. These responses ranged from 47 percent in the 3001 or more category to 71 percent in the 2001 to 3000 category.

The principal learning resources staff members were responsible to an academic dean in 58 percent of the colleges. Most of the others reported to a vice president or some other administrator having college-wide responsibilities. In each of the six regions, more than 52 percent of the principal staff members likewise reported to an academic dean. Three out of every four LRC administrators were employed on a twelve-month contract.

In more than 88 percent of 131 community colleges, the principal staff member was responsible for preparing the annual budget. This practice was also evident when comparing the responses by facility type. In the community colleges where the principal staff member did not have this responsibility, the dean, finance department, administrative committee, president, business manager, or vice-president was responsible for developing the annual budget. No matter what percentage of the total annual budget was allocated for learning resources, the greatest concentration of responses indicated that the principal learning resource staff member was responsible for budget preparation.

Support Personnel. Seven out of every ten colleges employed full-time (FT) clerks and/or technicians in the learning resources facility. More than half of these colleges employed between one and six full time clerks or technicians. Nine out of every ten colleges did not hire full time students, and eight out of every ten colleges did not hire full time aides or other types of support personnel.

TABLE 13

FREQUENCY DISTRIBUTION OF
TYPES OF PAID SUPPORT PERSONNEL

Number of Personnel	AIDES		CLERKS		TECHNICIANS		STUDENTS		OTHER	
	FT	PT	FT	PT	FT	PT	FT	PT	FT	PT
0	117	118	41	112	50	123	136	49	124	140
1–3	24	16	52	29	58	25	2	10	22	10
4–6	5	4	30	5	29	2	2	17	3	0
7–9	1	1	11	3	8	0	2	15	0	0
10–12	0	3	9	1	1	0	4	13	1	0
13–15	1	1	1	0	2	0	1	9	0	0
16 +	2	7	6	0	2	0	3	37	0	0
Total	150	150	150	150	150	150	150	150	150	150
No. of Colleges Employing Help	36	32	109	38	100	27	14	101	26	10
Average No. of Those Employing Help	5.0	7.6	5.5	2.7	3.9	1.6	12.1	17.0	2.2	1.4

More than 75 percent of the community colleges reported that they did not employ part-time (PT) aides, clerks, technicians, or other supportive staff. Approximately 68 percent indicated that they did employ part-time students. Community colleges that did employ part-time staff usually employed between one and three persons.

Colleges that employed students (37 percent) usually hired sixteen or more students. The 101 colleges that employed part-time students averaged seventeen students each.

Instructional Development Staff. Seventy-eight percent of the community colleges reported that they did not assign full time professional staff to instructional development activities. Of the 33 colleges having full time staff assigned, 31 reported that there were between one and five full time professional staff members assigned to instructional development activities.

The learning resources center facility type reported that 79 percent of them did not have full time professional staff assigned to instructional development activities. The media centers, central libraries, and audiovisual centers reported that between 90 and 100 percent had no one assigned to instructional development. The central library/audiovisual centers had 63 percent and the other facility type 86 percent of their colleges with professional staff assigned to instructional development activities.

Sixty-three percent of the community colleges responded that professional staff were assigned part-time to instructional development activities. Half of the colleges had one to five staff members assigned part-time to instructional development activities. The average number of persons assigned was 2.34 in each case.

Reviewing instructional development activities by facility type, colleges with learning resources centers and media centers reported that more than 60 percent of them have part-time professional staff to provide assistance in this area. Colleges having central libraries, audiovisual centers, central library–audiovisual centers, and other types stated that more than 57 percent of their colleges had no part-time professional staff assigned to instructional development activities.

Except for the western region, the colleges responded

overwhelmingly that no learning resources professional staff were assigned full time to instructional development activities. The percentages ranged from 100 percent in New England to 76 percent in the north central region. The 115 negative responses to this question represented 78 percent of the 148 responding colleges. The western region, however, showed that 40 percent had one to five learning resources professional staff assigned full time to instructional development activities.

Half of the colleges responding in each region assigned one to five learning resource professional staff part-time to instructional development activities. The range was from 50 percent in the southern and northwestern regions to 83 percent in the northeast region.

TABLE 14

FREQUENCY DISTRIBUTION OF STAFF ASSIGNED TO
INSTRUCTIONAL DEVELOPMENT ACTIVITIES

Staff	Professional	Non-professional
Part-time	63	29
Number Average	2.34	1.86
Full-time	22	13
Number Average	1.78	2.32

Professional staff were assigned part-time to instructional development activities more frequently than were non-professional staff. More than 60 percent of the professional staff were assigned part-time, while only 29 percent of the non-professional staff were assigned part-time.

In examining total staff, professional and non-professional, more were assigned part-time than full-time to instructional development activities. Full time assignments for professional staff occurred only 13 percent of the time.

Arrangement and Accessibility of Learning Resources

Materials. Of the 97 community colleges answering this question, 73 percent grouped materials by format and filed on open shelves. Fifty-seven percent of the central library–audiovisual center and other types, and a range of from 71 percent to 85 percent of the learning resources centers, media centers, and central libraries said that they group materials and file on open shelves. The audiovisual centers had a 100 percent positive response to this question.

Eight out of every ten community colleges responded that they did not interfile learning resources on open shelves. The central library, audiovisual center, and other facility types reported positive responses ranging from 33 percent to 50 percent. Community colleges with central library–audiovisual centers, and 10 out of 15 of those with media centers, did not interfile on open shelves. Seventeen percent of learning resources centers interfiled on open shelving.

Nine out of every ten community colleges made all materials easily accessible for use. All but one of the 150 community colleges stated that equipment was easily accessible for use within the learning resources facility. With two exceptions, equipment was accessible for classroom use, and there was provision for the preview of materials in the responding community colleges.

Faculty interlibrary loans were arranged in all but 2 of the responding 148 community colleges. Only 84 percent of the colleges arranged interlibrary loans for students.

Three out of every four community colleges used bulletins to inform staff about new acquisitions. Other methods, used less frequently, included sending materials to departments, displays, sending catalog cards or book catalogs to departments, and releases in campus newspapers.

In 85 percent of the colleges, the learning resources program served as a clearinghouse for all new material requests. New equipment requests were handled by 78 percent of the learning resources program.

TABLE 15

FREQUENCY DISTRIBUTION OF LEARNING RESOURCE PROGRAM
CLEARINGHOUSE FUNCTION BY FACILITY TYPE

Clearinghouse Function	LRC	MC	CL	AVC	CL-AVC	Other	Total
Materials	90	18	6	3	6	3	126
Equipment	87	15	3	3	3	3	114
Total Colleges	98	24	10	3	8	7	150

TABLE 16

FREQUENCY DISTRIBUTION OF PROFESSIONAL
COLLECTION BY FACILITY TYPE

Professional Collection	LRC	MC	CL	AVC	CL-AVC	Other	Total
Available	81	20	7	1	8	4	121
Not Available	17	4	3	2	0	3	29
Total	98	24	10	3	8	7	150

Nearly eight out of every ten of the colleges reported that a professional collection was available for faculty use. All of the central library–audiovisual centers have such collections.

Awareness of Program. More than eight out of every ten community colleges informed college personnel of collection holdings through bibliographies. Three out of every four colleges said they use orientation sessions to inform personnel about the LRC program. More than half of the colleges reported using displays, reports, inservice sessions, office meetings, and conferences.

The most frequent method of informing the administration of the learning resource program needs was through reports. More than 93 percent of the colleges used this method. Office meetings were used in more than 85 percent of the colleges. Some of the other methods used less frequently included budget requests, personal contacts, conferences, program proposals, and newsletters.

Collection Re-evaluation. "Newer Materials Available" was given as the most frequent reason for reevaluating the learning resources collection. Almost 97 percent of the colleges reported this. "Changing Curriculum Content" was also extensively used by 90 percent of the colleges as a trigger for evaluating their collections. "New Teaching Techniques" were considered by over 78 percent of the colleges in reevaluating their collections. Several other reasons for reevaluation included circulation, collections of nearby institutions, student/faculty demands, self-evaluation, new curriculum, and institutional objectives.

Handbooks. In two-thirds of the 150 colleges, a faculty handbook was available which described all facets of the learning resources program. Seven out of every ten colleges reported that student handbooks were available.

TABLE 17

FREQUENCY DISTRIBUTION OF LEARNING RESOURCES HANDBOOK
AVAILABILITY BY FACILITY TYPE

Type of Handbook	LRC	MC	CL	AVC	CL-AVC	Other	Total
Faculty	71	14	4	3	7	4	103
Student	76	18	5	0	6	3	108
Total Colleges	98	24	10	3	8	7	150

Policy statements governing the operation of the learning resources program were available for faculty, student, and administrative use in more than 80 percent of the colleges.

TABLE 18

FREQUENCY DISTRIBUTION OF LEARNING RESOURCES PROGRAM
POLICY STATEMENTS AVAILABILITY BY FACILITY TYPE

Policy Statements	LRC	MC	CL	AVC	CL-AVC	Other	Total
Available	81	17	6	3	8	5	120
Not Available	15	7	4	0	0	0	28
Total	96	24	10	3	8	7	148

Teaching Related Activities. Approximately 60 percent of the colleges reported that the learning resource program staff did present materials and/or information in classroom settings, thus providing an instructional service. More colleges included learning resources staff on teaching teams than did not in every facility type. The central library–audiovisual centers had the greatest percentage (75%) of their staff serving as teaching team members.

In the New England, southern, and north central regions, the responses regarding teaching team membership were evenly divided between "yes" and "no," with the northwest region indicating five "yes" to three "no" responses. The middle and western regions had a greater percentage of "yes" answers, with 71 percent and 73 percent respectively.

TABLE 19

FREQUENCY DISTRIBUTION OF LEARNING RESOURCES PROGRAM
STAFF MEMBERSHIP ON CURRICULUM COMMITTEES BY FACILITY TYPE

Curriculum Committee Members	LRC	MC	CL	AVC	CL-AVC	Other	Total
Yes	76	15	8	3	6	6	114
No	22	9	2	0	2	1	36
Total	98	24	10	3	8	7	150

Three-fourths of the responding community colleges reported that the staff of the learning resources program served on curriculum committees. The highest percentage (100 percent) of involvement was reported by the audiovisual centers, while the media centers had the lowest percentage (63 percent).

The learning resource professional staff served on curriculum committees in 66 to 80 percent of the colleges in the New England, southern, north central, and western regions. Only 50 percent of the staff in the northwest region served on curriculum committees, while in the middle region 90 percent did.

Nine colleges out of every ten agreed that planning with faculty members does keep the learning resources program staff informed about future assignments and needs. The range was from 79 percent of the media centers to 100 percent of the audiovisual centers and central library–audiovisual centers. Only 13 percent of the colleges felt their learning resources staff were heavily involved in planning curricular changes and teaching/learning innovations. The remaining colleges were evenly divided in their responses regarding curricular changes and innovations between slight (46 percent) and moderate (41 percent) involvement. There is some variation revealed when the data is analyzed by facility type.

TABLE 20

FREQUENCY DISTRIBUTION OF LEARNING RESOURCES PROGRAM STAFF
INVOLVEMENT IN CURRICULAR DEVELOPMENT ACTIVITIES BY FACILITY TYPE

Amount	LRC	MC	CL	AVC	CL-AVC	Other	Total
Slight	39	13	9	1	4	1	67
Moderate	45	6	1	2	2	4	60
Heavy	12	3	0	0	2	2	19
Total	96	22	10	3	8	7	146

There was less consistency among responses by regions to the question of involvement. Three regions (middle, southern, and northwest) had the greatest percentage of responses in the "slight" category. The other regions (New England, north central, and western) had their highest percentage of responses in the "moderate" category.

Cooperative Activities. More than three-fourths of the 146 colleges responding to this question reported that the staff of their learning resources program were involved in cooperative activities with other community groups and organizations through conferences and visits. Approximately one-third of the colleges reported involvement through reports, bibliographies, program exchange, and several other methods, including consortia, workshops, union lists of resources, loans of resources, speaker's bureaus, and professional organizations.

INSTRUCTIONAL SERVICES

Instructional Support. In this section of the questionnaire, twenty-two types of services are listed. The respondents were asked to check the learning resource program services that were, in their judgment, providing direct instructional support. The respondents were to indicate whether or not the services were (1) not provided, (2) provided to any faculty member, or (3) provided to the department. In the second and third sections of each question, the respondents were to indicate whether faculty or department use was (1) non-existent, (2) light, (3) medium, or (4) heavy. One of the purposes of questions 46–67 was to assist in selecting sites to visit which offered a range and variety of instructional services.

Since the majority of persons did not respond to department use of the various services, a discussion by department is excluded. It was indicated that since the service was provided directly to the faculty, the departments were also being served. However, individual responses are provided, see Appendix G. The discussion of faculty use is summarized by the extent of usage rather than question by question. Only those facility types for which responses differ greatly from the total are discussed in detail.

Of the twenty-two instructional services listed, six were provided to faculty members by more than 90 percent of the community colleges. The most popular services and the level of usage follow:

1. Ordering new print materials on request—medium to heavy usage

2. Having available audiodiscs or tape recordings, on request, for individuals for specific classes—medium to heavy usage

3. Having available visual materials, on request, for individual assignments for specific classes—medium to heavy usage

4. Producing audio recordings in any format—evenly divided between medium and heavy usage

5. Providing consultation on materials needed in special subject areas—medium to light usage

6. Providing instruction in the use of learning resources program—medium to light usage

Five additional faculty services had a response of from 80 to 89 percent, while six other services had responses of from 70 to 79 percent. Therefore, 77 percent of the services listed in the questionnaire were provided by more than 70 percent of the responding community colleges. These additional services and their usage provided by three-fourths or more of the colleges follow:

1. Ordering new nonprint materials on request—medium to heavy usage

2. Placing print materials on closed reserve for specific classes—medium to heavy usage

3. Producing copy slides or regular slide sets for use in instruction—medium to heavy usage

4. Producing overhead transparencies—even usage in all three categories: light, medium and heavy

5. Providing video tape recordings for individual viewing assignments for specific classes—medium to light usage

6. Providing consultation on resources needed for units of instruction—light and medium usage

7. Providing services whereby materials can be *adopted* to fill the college's instruction program—light and medium usage

8. Producing video tape recordings—light to medium usage

9. Providing guidance in listening/viewing—light to medium usage

10. Preparing special bibliographies on request—light usage

11. Providing services whereby materials can be *adapted*

to fill the college's instructional program—light usage

Two-thirds of the colleges provided production of learning packages and experienced generally light usage.

Approximately one-third of the colleges offered the following three services and reported either light or non-existent usage:

1. Observing students in the center for purposes of sharing with faculty information about interests, needs, and habits of study and reading behavior
2. Providing a program whereby instructional materials and methods can be evaluated according to their teaching effectiveness
3. Providing a listing of community resources which support the college's instructional program

The production of computer-assisted instruction programs was little used. Only 18 of the 143 colleges responding provided this service; eleven of these 18 colleges have learning resources centers. The remaining 7 are two with media centers, two with central libraries, and three with other facility types.

The learning resources centers, media centers, audiovisual centers, and central library–audiovisual center responses to these twenty-two statements on instructional services were very similar to those for the total population. The central libraries showed only ten of the services being offered by more than 70 percent of their colleges. The other types of facilities had the lowest percentage of colleges providing any one service.

INSTRUCTIONAL DEVELOPMENT

Resource Assistance. Nine out of ten community colleges

responded that staff of the learning resources program work with faculty members by assisting them with the integration of instructional resources into their teaching activities. Almost 80 percent of the colleges responded that assistance is provided for individual faculty members as well as departments and units.

Four methods of assisting faculty with integrating instructional resources which were used by more than 50 percent of the colleges include—

1. assistance given on a "first-come-first-served" basis;
2. assistance not charged to the individual or instructional unit since the budget of the learning resources program was sufficient to cover all costs;
3. assistance given in the production and use of materials which were used outside the learning resources program facilities; and
4. assistance provided faculty members in all phases of producing learning packages.

Assistance given according to number of students; assistance given to departments or units only, not to individual faculty members; assistance given for required courses as a priority over elective courses; and cost of assistance willingly shared by faculty or departments or units: all of these have a very low incidence of response (1 to 3 percent). Eight of the twelve responses to these four areas are from the learning resources center facility type.

Instructional Areas Using Learning Resources. When the LRC administrators were asked: "In your judgment, what are the specific departments or courses in which your learning resources program has had the greatest effect directly on instruction?", they indicated as a group that twenty-seven different subject areas were making extensive instructional related use of the LRC. Several of the responses are grouped for ease in reporting.

The fields of health careers (43 percent), social studies (43 percent), science (41 percent), language arts (31 percent), business (24 percent), humanities (21 percent), fine arts (17 percent), mathematics (12 percent), foreign languages (7 percent), and vocational education (5 percent) were making the greatest use of the learning resources program. The remaining seventeen areas, with four or fewer responses, include architecture, automotive programs, agriculture, cosmetology, counseling, drafting, electronics, engineering technology, home economics, landscaping, law enforcement programs, library/media technology, mechanics, physical education, public and community services, real estate, and veterinary science.

Instructional Support Success. Three major success factors were identified in the nineteen different responses to "What was considered your greatest success in supporting or influencing instruction?":

1. "Learning resources personnel and faculty cooperation are important in supporting or influencing instruction" was thought to be a true statement by 39 percent of the colleges. Of the colleges which felt that this was true, 60 percent had a program of the learning resources center facility type.
2. "Offering a full range of services" was the second most important supporting factor for 26 percent of the colleges.
3. Third most frequently mentioned as a service important in supporting or influencing instruction was "media design, development, and production." Mentioned by 20 percent of the colleges, 23 percent of those with learning resources centers ascribed their success in

the instructional area to this service.

"Individualized instruction" was mentioned by 7 percent of the colleges as a success factor. The remaining 15 items had five or fewer responses. These included mediated instruction, administrative support, student use and involvement, and public relations.

Instructional Support Difficulties. The 148 responding colleges listed nineteen major difficulties in supporting or influencing instruction. Four of them were experienced by more than 16 percent of the colleges.

Approximately one-third of the colleges mentioned budget difficulties and constraints.

Faculty resistance to change was the second most frequently mentioned problem with one out of four of the community colleges citing this as a difficulty. This resistance to change and unwillingness by the faculty to use a wider variety of media and new methods plagued all six facility types.

The third most frequently mentioned difficulty was an insufficient number of learning resources staff. Nearly one-fifth of the community colleges mentioned this as a problem. Notable numbers of responses appeared in the learning resources center, central library, and central library-audiovisual center facility types.

More than 16 percent of the colleges indicated that limited faculty was also a major difficulty. From this point on, the responses to other difficulties represented less than 9 percent of the total population. Some of these additional difficulties included: lack of administrative support and disinterested attitude, lack of sufficient time, use of traditional instruction, and inadequate facilities.

A conclusion to be drawn from the above data, is that many learning resources programs are providing exemplary services which are supportive of community college instructional activities. The information reveals that the learning resources programs are not tied to the more traditional aspects of librarianship. As a matter of fact it appears that their very existence depends upon their willingness to experiment, adopt, and adapt information services which will provide teaching and learning assistance.

Chapter VI
Report of Site Visits

OVERVIEW

The information contained in this chapter comes directly from visits to each of the seven community colleges selected for site observation. Profiles of each of the colleges are to be found in Appendix H. The visits brought into focus a picture of current community college learning resources programs and interviews with learning resources center administrators, learning resources center staff members, college administrators, faculty members, and students provided descriptive information which could be collected only in this manner.*

The seven community colleges were chosen to provide a respresentative sampling of elements which are thought to be desirable for a sound learning resources program. The criteria used to select the site visit locations are outlined in the Introduction. The numerous elements considered essential for the learning resources programs are organized in various ways and in varying proportions but the factor which appears in all successful programs is the ability of the learning resources center staff to be people-oriented and to work with various groups and individuals.

*The information provided describes the programs as they were at the time of the visits. Many changes have occurred, yet the data still illustrates models around which instructionally oriented learning resources programs can be developed.

135

The information collected is reported according to "very similar," "similar," and "dissimilar" responses. Thirteen of the 19 questions asked provided "very similar" responses, two questions had "similar" responses, and four questions had "dissimilar" responses.

A conclusion which can be drawn from the responses is that, even though community colleges have diverse settings and administrative patterns, many similarities exist in those which provide a comprehensive learning resources program related to innovative instruction. These similarities are reported in the following paragraphs.

The characteristics of the learning resources staff were similar. Staff members tended to be young, work well with people, and have a master's degree and previous library experience in either public schools, public libraries, or academic libraries. The staff were involved in the development and support of the college's educational programs through consultative services and direct teaching activities.

Since the services provided by the learning resources center affect innovative instruction, it is necessary for a good relationship to exist between the learning resources program staff and the faculty involved in innovative instructional programs. Many of the learning resources center services directly impact upon innovative instructional activities. Perhaps the most important of these services is consultation with faculty and the creation of an environment conducive to innovative instruction. Also very important is the provision of equipment and assistance for locally produced instructional materials.

In order for a comprehensive learning resources program to aid innovative instruction, it is mandatory that all forms of media be readily available. Nearly all instructional areas in the seven colleges visited were using a wide variety of media and materials. All learning resources center administrators indicated that innovation requires better use of existing technology and materials than does traditional instruction.

Despite the importance of innovation on each of the campuses, the process for initiating innovation was unsystematic. Several colleges did allow release time for development, and three colleges budgeted money for instructional development services. A review procedure for newly designed courses was used by each college.

The majority of faculty on each campus were involved in the learning resources program. Methods for involving faculty which were observed were:

1. Faculty helped select and use materials necessary for instructional development projects.
2. Faculty served on college-wide committees which relate to the learning resources program and were involved in many forms of informal exchange of ideas.
3. Faculty committed to innovative instructional programs regard media as a priority item.

One result of a comprehensive learning resources program was that faculty use of media increased. This increase was due in part to the fact that with a greater variety of learning resources available there was a change in the instructional approach. During discussions with various faculty members, a majority expressed the view that an increase in the use of media would continue. They also believed that their use of media would become more sophisticated.

Learning resources program advisory committees existed in five of the colleges. These committees encouraged communication between the learning resources center staff and the faculty or departments they represent.

There was little evidence of a systematic approach to evaluation of the learning resources center services. Most assessment was done on an informal basis. Administrators felt that it is important to keep an open atmosphere and a good relationship with the faculty so this informal evaluation could continue. However, these informal approaches were frequently not sufficient to permit the consistent and necessary collection and reporting of program results and accomplishments.

Technological systems were used on all of the community college campuses. The learning resources centers were using data processing for administrative and managerial operations. Most centers were involved in radio programming, and all centers were involved with television production. Several colleges were using computer-assisted instruction.

Nearly half of the students interviewed used the learning resources center daily, and another 40 percent used the center on a weekly basis. Students were most frequently able to find the information they needed. Most requests were class-related; however, the requests for recreational and self-interest materials were increasing.

The greatest variance occurred in the area of planning documents. Short-range plans were found in all colleges, but long-range plans were found in only four of the seven colleges. Five colleges prepared annual reports. The contents of these documents varied but the objectives were similar—to enlarge the scope and effectiveness of the learning resources program.

Learning resources centers, in community colleges, have typically developed in one of the following three ways: (1) as unified programs, (2) as expanded library services, and (3) as a combination of existing library and audiovisual services. Faculty, staff, and administrators indicated that the LRC was the best means for assisting in instructional development.

The administrative patterns of the learning resources programs were all quite different and the title of the person responsible for the program varied. However, invariably, the program administrator was a member of the college's administrative staff.

The learning resources centers were all involved in cooperative interagency activities. The types of activities varied greatly—from materials borrowing to the exchange of locally developed instructional programs. Several colleges were cooperating in intrastate projects.

DOCUMENTATION

During the visits, an attempt was made to observe as many different aspects of the learning resources program as possible. The following responses to the questions, found in the Site Visitation Questionnaire (Appendix H), provide a detailed descriptive statement of activities found at the time of the visits.

The learning resources staff were asked fourteen questions, the faculty three questions, and two were directed to students. The responses are reported as "very similar" (six or seven colleges), "similar" (five colleges), and "dissimilar" (four or less colleges). Responses are "very similar" to thirteen of the nineteen questions, while two responses are "similar" and four are "dissimilar."

VERY SIMILAR RESPONSES

Learning Resources Center Staff and the Educational Program

The staffs of all seven learning resources programs were deeply involved in the development and delivery of the colleges' instructional programs. In six of the seven colleges, the professional staff of the learning resources program held faculty rank and status. In the one institution where faculty rank was not granted, the learning resources center staff were considered professional staff and could be given multi-year contracts.

All seven of the colleges had professional LRC staff

assigned to instructional development activities, broken down as: (1) consultative services and (2) direct teaching activities.

1. Consultative services, which were provided through—
    a. resource acquisitions,
    b. service and program awareness activities with faculty,
    c. programs on equipment and material use,
    d. production services,
    e. previewing services, and
    f. instructional development activities;

2. Direct teaching activities, including—
    a. inservice programs for teaching and administrative personnel,
    b. graduate credit courses relating to the use of media taught by local college personnel and held in the LRC,
    c. working with faculty on a one-to-one or small group basis,
    d. library media technology programs taught by some LRC staff,
    e. overload teaching assignments, and
    f. instructing a unit or portion of an existing course in which an LRC staff member has expertise.

All seven of the administrators stated that their position in administration has a bearing on the effectiveness of the learning resources center program and its relationship to the instructional program. Six of the seven administrators of the learning resources program met frequently with fellow administrators for the purposes of designing curricular change, establishing campus-wide policies and procedures, and planning future directions for all college-wide programs. Members of the learning resources center staff were actively involved in faculty affairs. A number of LRC staff had served on negotiation teams, as officers of faculty committees, and as representatives to state and national associations.

The administrators expressed concern that there was still need for further development of the learning resources center staff's involvement in the educational program. One administrator said: "There exists the need for selling the learning resources program through an active public awareness campaign. The learning resources center staff needs to talk with the total college community." When this is accomplished, there will be greater and more extensive ties between the learning resources center program and the educational program within the community college field.

LEARNING RESOURCES PROGRAM AND INNOVATIVE INSTRUCTIONAL PROGRAMS

The relationship of the learning resources program to innovative instructional programs, at least in concept, was consistent among the seven campuses. The administrators of the program stated that making materials and equipment conveniently accessible for faculty use is extremely important in supporting innovative instructional activities; availability of local production services was also considered important. To assist faculty in this area, two colleges had provided facilities where faculty could produce their own materials.

The process of relating the learning resources program to innovative instructional practices is never rigid; it is a process in which constant flexibility is inherent. Examples of this process:

1. Once faculty have planned their course syllabus and appropriate content, learning resources support services are requested.

2. Learning resources center staff shares ideas and resources with faculty.

3. Learning resources center staff has specific responsibility for working with faculty members involved in instructional change, i.e., as media utilization consultants or advisors and instructional technologists.

4. The administrator of the learning resources program serves on curriculum and other campus-wide committees, so as to provide ideas on innovations.

5. A portion of the learning resources center budget is set aside for innovative projects.

Two learning resources administrators voiced differing opinions as to provision of services which support innovative instructional activites. One claimed that all functions providing direct campus-wide instructional support should be included in the learning resources program. The other stated that there was danger in making the learning resources center too inclusive, that the learning resources center should remain purely a service agency and leave instructional design and development to others. However, in the opinion of the writer, if instruction is going to include the use of media as a core component, then the learning resources staff must play a major role in instructional development.

There was a positive relationship between the learning resources program and innovative instructional programs. The process varied greatly, but many instructional areas were making effective use of a variety of learning resources. The following are specific components of the learning resources program which supported innovative practices:

1. television services

2. independent learning activities
3. developmental learning laboratories
4. 16mm film distribution services
5. audio-tutorial laboratories
6. computer-assisted instruction
7. computer-managed instruction
8. video taping
9. slide/tape packaging
10. filmstrip collections
11. print materials collection

SERVICES PROVIDED RELATING TO
INNOVATIVE INSTRUCTION

On all seven campuses, some services being provided by
the learning resources center staff directly related to innovative instruction. Three LRC administrators stated the
case more strongly, affirming that all services provided
related to innovative instruction. The learning resources
program had established an open environment, placing few
obstacles between the patron and needed resources. This atmosphere resulted in continued growth and support of the
learning resources program.

The following two charts are taken from the *Learning
Resource Center Handbook*, 1974, of Lane Community
College, Eugene, Oregon. The charts describe the types of
services offered by the Learning Resources Center staff
which support instructional innovation. The services
described in the two charts are being provided in various
ways by the learning resources programs of the other six
community colleges, depending on their organizational
structures.

Additional services provided in this area are:
1. Faculty consultation
2. Flexible approach to instructional development

The LRC assists in the evaluation of existing programs and design of new curriculum.

Library
* Bibliographic services (book)
* Assist with research and reference
* ERIC materials
* Print and micro-print media resource assistance

Audio visual
* Bibliographic service (non-book)
* Types of equipment available (some photographic production)
* Resource assistance for nonprint materials in curriculum design
* Facilities design for media usage

Electronic Production
* Audio and video production on and off campus
* Re-play audio and video through IRS
* Resource person for video program development
* Facilities design for video usage
* Live classroom transmission

Printing-Graphics
* Resource for production of workbooks, manuals, brochures, handbooks, etc.
* Resource for production of visuals for projection, charts, maps, diagrams, schematics, etc.

Study Skills Learning Center
* Staff resources — design and develop small group and individually prescribed instruction (remedial through accelerated programs).

Instructional Technology
* Curriculum development, media design and evaluation
* Proposal writing — consulting, personalized instruction

This assumes adequate personnel to perform these services, particularly bibliography service and reference service.

FIGURE 4:
LRC SUPPORT SERVICES ROLE IN
CURRICULUM DEVELOPMENT

LRC

ARCHIVES | SECRETARY / CLERK

	S. Skills	Lib.	AVS	EP	P/G	Inst. Tech.
	Reading English as a Second Language Labs Effective Learning	Technical Proc. Reference Circulation Reserve Serials Interlibrary Loan Microfilm Cassette Programmed instructional materials	Circulation • Equipment • Materials Film Rental Equipment • Evaluation* • Purchases Materials • Evaluation* • Purchases Film Production Audio Cassette Duplication Programmed Materials	Internal Retrieval System Community Cable Television Video • Production • Duplication Audio • Production • Duplication Microwave	Printing Photo Composition Collating Drilling Cutting Padding Graphics • Design • Photography • Plate making • Laminating • Transparencies	Curriculum Media & Program Evaluation Consulting Proposal Writing Independent Study Individualized Instruction
Orientation	Student service	Staff and student service	Staff service	Staff and student service	Staff service	Staff service

* In conjunction with the instructional technologist

S. Skills - Study Skills Learning Center
Lib. - Library
AVS - Audiovisual Services

EP - Electronic Production
P/G - Printing Graphics
Inst. Tech. - Instructional Technology

FIGURE 5

SERVICES PROVIDED BY VARIOUS AREAS WITHIN THE LEARNING RESOURCES CENTER PROGRAM

3. Community services
4. Information retrieval system
5. Computer-assisted learning center
6. Media production areas
7. Career guidance information project
8. Book catalog
9. Integrated media on open shelves

On six of the campuses, the learning resources program supported learning labs, which were located in various divisions throughout the college. Most of the materials provided in the learning labs were commercially prepared; however, more and more locally produced packages were being developed. On the seventh campus, which does not heavily support divisional learning laboratories, an instructional media area was being developed within the learning resources center. This was planned to house a listening/viewing area with carrels and appropriate equipment.

From the range and variety of service provided on each of the seven college campuses, it was concluded that the learning resources program was performing as an instructional service agency. One of the LRC directors summarized the relationship of the learning resources center's services to innovative instruction by claiming that "innovative ideas are given a chance to live. Teaching faculty have led, pulled, pushed the learning resources staff and vice versa."

FACULTY INVOLVEMENT IN THE DEVELOPMENT OF THE LEARNING RESOURCES CENTER PROGRAM

Administrators of the learning resources programs stated that the majority of faculty members were very supportive and committed to the use of the learning resources program. One administrator emphasized that during budget cutbacks, the faculty's support caused the learning resources

budget to be increased in order to provide needed resources
and instructional services. Six of the seven administrators indicated that between 33 to 98 percent of the faculty regularly used the LRC program.

There are numerous ways the faculty had become involved in the development of the learning resources center's program. Some of these are:

1. Faculty often suggest topics or specific titles of new
   materials to be purchased, although the final selection
   decisions rest with the learning resources program
   staff.
2. On a regular basis, more than 50 percent of the faculty
   request or produce instructional materials from the
   production unit.
3. Schedules of the learning resources staff provide time
   to be spent with faculty members in planning methods
   of using materials in their teaching.
4. Faculty and learning resources staff establish an open
   relationship which is developed through cooperative
   activities, such as meetings with division chairpersons,
   individual or group staff conferences, workshops, and
   committee meetings.
5. Faculty involvement is also influenced by the physical
   size of the college and the location of the learning
   resources program in relation to other instructional
   areas.

EVALUATION OF THE
LEARNING RESOURCES PROGRAM SERVICES

The procedures used for the continuous evaluation of the
services provided by the staff of the learning resources program were staff and product oriented. Other than staff
evaluations, most other assessment/evaluation was done on

an informal basis. Six of the seven colleges had a formalized staff performance evaluation process. The openness of the learning resources programs in six institutions enabled the student, faculty, staff, and college administrators to provide, on a systematic basis, input regarding the effectiveness of the learning resources program. During discussions with LRC administrators, it was revealed that very little substantial systematic evaluation of services was done. Statistical information was kept in all seven institutions. Two colleges used computers extensively to analyze the collected data.

User questionnaires and surveys had been developed and used on four of the seven campuses. Administrators of three of these four programs thought that the results received were not extremely useful. Few persons respond to a formalized approach, so an informal way of gathering information was believed to be more effective.

FACULTY USE OF
MEDIATED INSTRUCTION

According to statistics examined during the visits, the proportion of community college faculty using mediated instruction had increased over the previous three years. All seven of the institutions reported that more and more faculty were relying on the use of media, an indication that mediated instruction will continue to grow. Over the three years, there had been more opportunities for faculty in all seven colleges to have practical, media-related experiences which resulted in improved student learning rates and comprehension.

The LRC administrators stated that after concentrated work with several faculty members, they were able to encourage other staff members to incorporate media into their instructional programs. There remained a small number of faculty members who would never use media, but for the majority, media had become an integral part of teaching. The faculty who do use media have found teaching to be more rewarding for they were better able to satisfy the variety of instructional needs presented by students.

Types of services included in mediated instruction which had experienced the greatest increase over the three-year period were (1) local production, (2) listening/viewing, (3) graphics, (4) computer-assisted instruction, and (5) video taping.

FACULTY ANTICIPATED USE OF MEDIATED INSTRUCTION

The administrators of the seven programs were in agreement that the proportion of faculty members using mediated instruction would increase over the next three years. Reasons for this projection were based upon the following:

1. Media were being used extensively and becoming a way of life.

2. Media use could only increase, since more and more teachers used media or were "ready to jump into the media bag."

3. Inservice staff development opportunities were provided in the basic, as well as the more advanced, innovative techniques of media utilization.

4. College administrators were becoming committed to and encouraging the use of media.

5. Faculty members were encouraged and reimbursed for taking courses in media use offered at area colleges and

universities.

6. Faculty were becoming more conservative than they had been ten years ago. In returning to more traditional teaching, staff were extremely receptive to trying new techniques and strategies for the use of all types of media.

7. Emphasis was being placed upon the use and development of learning materials as a portion of the evaluation process.

8. Production staff were becoming more involved in assisting faculty members in planning, designing, and producing learning materials for classroom use.

9. Statistical information illustrated a growth pattern in the use of media—print materials, 16mm films, slides, transparencies, video and audio tapes, television programming, and information retrieval systems.

10. All units within the learning resources program were experiencing an increase in the number of requests for services.

11. There was increased use of commercially prepared materials in addition to a growing interest in locally produced materials.

In spite of these optimistic remarks, several cautionary statements must be made. If learning resource services decline, staff will stop using the learning resources program. There are constraints which may place barriers between the learning resources program and the user: (1) decreasing budgets, which result in lack of materials and limited staff and (2) inadequate facilities.

The types of mediated resources for which use was expected to increase were as follows:

1. Use of 16mm films will continue to grow as the most heavily used type of media.

2. Video taping will account for a considerable portion of the increased growth in mediated instruction. The bulk of taping will be done on location; however, studio taping will increase at a slower rate.

3. Slide/tape packages and transparencies will receive greater use because of ease of local production.

4. Microforms will become extensively used in community colleges. Back issues of periodicals and specialized materials are readily available on microform.

5. Locally produced audio cassettes will receive greater use. Their ease of distribution makes them more flexible than previously developed systems, such as the listening center.

TECHNOLOGICAL SYSTEMS USED

At the colleges visited, technological systems were a part of the learning resources program. A number of these systems or services were located in, or supported by, the learning resources center, including:

1. Computer-assisted instruction was being used in four institutions. In two other colleges, plans were being developed, whereby CAI would be added as an instructional strategy. The content areas using computer-assisted instruction were general science, social studies,

math, sociology, physics, dental health, remedial math and English, English-as-a-Second-Language, library technology, and nursing programs.

2. Data processing was used as an administrative tool in all seven colleges. In five institutions, the learning resources programs were using data processing. Services consisted of on-line circulation, reports, generation of bibliographies, inventory control, evaluation information, statistical record keeping, and catalogs.

3. Dial access, as a technological system, drew one of the most varied responses among the seven sites. Three colleges had planned for the installation of a system within the learning resources center. One center never installed the system due to a negative faculty reaction. The other two colleges installed a system, one of which later sold it to another institution. The only college which had an operational retrieval system had made extensive use of it. Its listing of programs were both commercially and locally prepared, and the offerings were constantly being expanded according to instructional and user needs.

   A major reason for the lack of interest in dial access is that the needs of a commuter campus could not be served by a non-portable system. Cassettes have replaced dial access systems by providing a more flexible and transportable service.

4. Five community colleges had campus radio stations or access to air time on locally owned stations. In two institutions, plans were underway to provide a limited number of courses via the radio.

5. Six of the seven colleges had campus production facilities for locally produced television programming.

Three of the facilities were within the learning resources program, while the remaining three were in the areas of mass communications or broadcasting. Three campuses had full color production studios. Two of the other colleges were considering the installation of color capability. Two of the colleges used video tapes as their distribution systems, while the other four colleges had campus-wide closed circuit system.

The one institution without campus facilities had produced three programs in cooperation with two national television networks. Video cassettes served as their local distribution system.

6. Two learning resources programs were providing work processing services. This provided an alternative to limited secretarial assistance within each campus-wide program area.

CHARACTERISTICS OF THE LEARNING RESOURCES STAFF

The learning resources staff was a fairly homogeneous group. In six of the seven colleges, the staff was relatively young. Six of the colleges required a master's degree for all professional positions.

The job experiences of the learning resources staff prior to entering the community college field were quite diverse. Four of the seven administrators stated that the majority of their staff came from the public schools. Other staff members had received their experience in public libraries, college (including community college) and academic libraries, special libraries, and graduate schools.

Job descriptions for professional learning resources staff existed in four of the seven community colleges. These

descriptive statements were contained in a policy/proce-
dures manual. Since the LRC staff were members of the
faculty, most faculty handbooks contain general statements
applicable to them.

The LRC administrators indicated that the learning
resources staff were people who know how to work well
with others. This skill enabled them to sell the learning
resources program successfully.

INSTRUCTIONAL STAFF AND THE LEARNING RESOURCES PROGRAM

The instructional staff of each college had played an important role in the development of the learning resources
program. The following are several examples of ways in
which this increasingly important role of faculty involvement had been achieved.

1. An open atmosphere in the learning resources center
   had encouraged the exchange of ideas, requests for
   services, and more frequent use of resources by the
   faculty. The faculty knew that they were encouraged
   to request resources and services.

2. In all of the colleges, the faculty indicated that in each
   term they were making more extensive use of learning
   resources. Most faculty included media as a priority
   item and an essential element in instructional planning.

3. The faculty of three colleges said that the learning
   resources center advisory committee was a positive factor for providing input into the development of the
   program. Input from other college-wide committees
   and meetings was also a valuable mechanism for chan-

neling information.

4. Three institutions had full-time staff assigned as material utilization specialists or instructional technologists. Through cooperative activities involving these individuals, it was thought that the learning resources program would continue to grow and meet the needs of the instructional staff.

5. In five of the seven institutions, the faculty stated that after they have roughly designed what they wanted to do, the learning resources staff then became involved and assisted in finalizing the new course of study or program.

6. During the faculty interviews, most expressed the belief that, as success was gained in one program, it would cause growth and expansion in other areas. Faculty usually asked what was available rather than what could be purchased or developed; therefore, instructional development reflected existing services and collections. This, too, was changing, although not as rapidly as instructional designers would like or hope.

Innovative teaching practices which were currently in use, or were being considered, at the time of the visits utilized all media formats and were found in all subject areas. The LRC administrators said that innovative teaching has a direct relationship to media usage and implies the better use of existing technology and materials. For example, in one college, faculty members designed instructional programs, learning packages, courses with open entry/exit options, and programmed learning materials. Innovative teaching was a natural outcome. This college had a national reputation in the area of instructional innovation and faculty were encouraged to design instructional programs which incorporate innovative practices.

The following descriptive information is illustrative of the types of innovative programs found in various curricular areas. Throughout all seven site visits, students and faculty members were observed using media.

1. *Study Skill Centers or Laboratories.* In the colleges visited, examples could be found in nearly all curricular areas. The following list is illustrative of the wide variety of centers which existed: hotel/motel management, horticulture, math, business, social studies, and home economics. One college had established a developmental laboratory committee responsible for coordinating all related activities. The learning resources program had representation on this committee.
   a. On all seven campuses, independent study centers had been established. These centers usually supported one curricular area. Depending upon the curricular area, the centers served varying teaching purposes—enrichment, reinforcement, tutorial, or basic instruction.
   b. A communications skill center had been developed on one campus. The center contained locally produced learning packages on language arts, which were primarily used by students enrolled in the technical/vocational program.
   c. Another campus had developed an extensive study skills center as part of the learning resources program. The primary focus of the center was to provide learning assistance to students in reading and study skills. The center contained instructional materials in math, foreign languages, nursing, history, science, music, and business.

d. On another campus, a learning skills project had been developed outside the learning resources center. The purpose of the project was to provide instructional services in the areas of identifying learning problems, counseling, providing basic or advanced tutorial assistance, and coordinating program activities with the teaching staff.

e. Career information centers, which were developed in cooperation with the learning resources program, had been established at three of the community colleges. Two of the centers used computerized programs for data retrieval.

f. One college had created a developmental learning laboratory. The laboratory provided students the opportunity to use a wide variety of materials with a variety of levels of learning difficulty. Media used in the laboratory were computer programs, programmed learning materials, audio tapes, slides, filmstrips, and printed materials.

g. Nursing education laboratories had been developed on all seven campuses. The focus of these laboratories was skills development through hands-on experiences and technically oriented knowledge received through the exchange of concepts and information. These centers extensively used media in most formats. One college was using a number of PLATO's (Programmed Logic for Automatic Teaching Operation's) computerized programs. Simulated exercises were incorporated into all programs visited.

h. One campus had established an instructional laboratory which housed developmental and technical learning materials. The three instruction areas which most heavily used the laboratory were nursing, secretarial science, and engineering technology.

2. *Health Related Programs*. In addition to the learning centers established in the nursing programs, there were a number of examples of innovative teaching practices in health related programs. The dental health program in one college had developed learning resource packages. The radiologic technology program in another college had made extensive use of video cassettes.

3. *Career/Technical Programs*. Law enforcement courses on three campuses used media. The video tape recorder was used for location shooting, which was later used for classroom simulation activities. One program made extensive use of 16mm films in classroom instruction.

   The fire prevention courses in one campus used portable video taping equipment for recording material for later classroom use. This was found to be a most effective means for simulating real life experiences for student discussion and analysis.

   The business division in one college had developed open entry/exit programs in the areas of shorthand, typing, and office practices. The office practices courses in another college consisted of self-paced individualized training units.

   Another college was invovled in a tri-state regional television project. The project, focussed on the teaching of middle-management techniques, was aimed at inservice training for public employees. The program was to be distributed via cable television. The college faculty was planning and developing the series while a commercial television network provided design and production services.

   Other career/technical courses using innovative teaching practices included—

    a. marketing courses, which used television for viewing selling practices and techniques;

    b. a manufacturing technology program, which had developed a slide/tape package, presenting an orientation to this program area;

    c. a data processing course which used a 16mm film on the five basic components of a computer system;

    d. air frame and power plant courses, which had developed open entry/exit programs;

    e. a home economics course, which had developed a slide/tape orientation package;

    f. engineering programs which used simulation activities;

    g. an electronics technology program which had developed a self-paced individualized instruction program for first-year students; and

    h. library media technology courses which used media extensively for teaching basic skill, reenforcement, and simulation activities.

4. *Physical Science.* Individualized instructional packages, video tapes, slide/tape packages, transparencies, filmstrips, 8mm film loops, and television programs were used extensively in science instruction. Three colleges had developed audio tutorial biology laboratory programs.

5. *Physical Education/Recreation.* Faculty members teaching various courses in physical education made extensive use of media. Because of heavy use and demand, one college had loaned a small collection of materials to the department for a skills development area. During site visitation students were observed using a single concept film loop on skiing techniques in a viewing center which had been set up in the equip-

ment room.

6. *Humanities*. Foreign language departments were making great use of audio tapes in all seven colleges. Tapes have been extremely effective in English-as-a-Second-Language programs, and one college is using computer programs on career planning for students learning English-as-a-Second-Language. The 16mm film had been widely used in foreign language instruction. Most LRC administrators stated that English programs make extensive use of all media. Individualized instructional materials, video tapes, slide/tape packages, audio tapes, 16mm films, and discs were the most frequently used types of media.

The speech and communications courses, as might be expected, made tremendous use of media. In three of the colleges, the campus-wide television production and distribution facilities were a part of the communication/broadcasting department. Close cooperation existed between the learning resources staff and the instructional personnel in all six institutions which had television studios.

7. *Math*. Types of media being used in math classrooms were audio tapes, video tapes, television programs, transparencies, individualized instructional packages, and remedial programs via the computer.

8. *Social Studies*. Social studies faculty members used slide/tape packages, discs, 16mm films, transparencies, filmstrips, and video tapes. One faculty member had developed two television series which were done in cooperation with two national commercial television networks.

Psychology instructors in one college used commercial television programs for case study work. The psychology department in another institution made extensive use of individualized instructional packages.

Several additional items indicated that other innovative teaching practices were in use on community college campuses. One learning resources director stated that he has a listing of nearly forty-five projects requesting learning resources center staff assistance. Two colleges prepared newsletters which summarize instructional development activities. Such dissemination instruments provide insight into new and innovative ideas and helped to spread ideas.

One college was studying the possibility of installing a high speed television distribution system with the capability of transmitting ten hours of programming in six minutes. The college felt that the system had almost unlimited potential for distributing television instruction to branch campuses and other instructional locations.

One college was planning a homebound telelecture program. Regularly scheduled classes were to be broadcast for students unable to attend regularly scheduled classes on campus.

Another college was studying the possibility of providing courses over the college's FM radio station. At the time of the site visits three courses were being designed for airing. If cable television were available in the area, it would be a better alternative and would have greater appeal for transmitting courses to homebound students.

CLASS-RELATED STUDENT USE OF THE LEARNING RESOURCES PROGRAM

Students were observed using instructional materials for class-related assignments. During the seven site visits, students were interviewed in the learning resources centers, lounge areas, halls, and various other places about their use of the learning resources program. On only one visit there was not a sufficient number of students available to talk with to obtain from them opinions relative to their use of the center. This was because the visit took place during a period of faculty inservice and student registration. The statistical information provided by the director of the program, however, indicated that the center was heavily used by both students and faculty.

During the other six visits, 171 students were asked about their class-related use of the learning resources program. Table 21 indicates the statistical information received.

TABLE 21

FREQUENCY OF STUDENT USE
OF THE LEARNING RESOURCES CENTERS

	DAILY		WEEKLY		MONTHLY		TOTAL	
Frequency	#	%	#	%	#	%	#	%
Students	81	47.4	69	40.3	21	12.3	171	100.0

In all of the visits, students and faculty were observed making use of the learning resources program. The main reading areas were crowded with patrons doing many types of information-related activities, and the physical facilities appeared to be adequate for the number of patrons using the centers in four of the seven colleges. The total space available in the learning resources programs ranged from 7.2 to 23.2 square feet per pupil.

ABILITY TO FIND NEEDED INFORMATION

When using the collection of the learning resources program, students were most frequently able to find their needed information. Table 22 indicates the responses made by the 171 students who were asked about this during the site visits.

TABLE 22

STUDENT RESPONSES FOR ABILITY TO
LOCATE NEEDED INFORMATION WITHIN THE
LEARNING RESOURCES COLLECTION

Frequency of Use	ABILITY TO LOCATE RESOURCES				
	Never	Seldom	Frequently	Always	Total
Daily	0	13	55	13	81
Weekly	1	11	43	14	69
Monthly	1	4	12	4	21
Total	2	28	110	31	171

The six colleges where mechanical counting devices had been installed indicated that the number of persons entering the center increased each month. Along with this fact, the learning resources center staffs reported that students and faculty made greater use of the collections and services once they were able to locate needed resources. Also, having adequate numbers of staff available to assist the user had helped to increase the effectiveness of the LRC program.

In the one institution where classes were not in session, the learning resources center staff indicated that the majority of student use was class-related. However, students were beginning to request materials and assistance in locating recreational and personal interest items. From circulation and use records kept, it is safe to say the patrons were able to fulfill their informational needs.

SIMILAR RESPONSES

LEARNING RESOURCES PROGRAM
ADVISORY COMMITTEE

There was a committee which served in an advisory

capacity to the learning resources center staff in five of the seven sites. The purposes of the advisory committees can be summarized as follows. The committees made recommendations for the improvement of services which support the instructional program, suggested procedures for evaluating the effectiveness of services rendered, recommended policies which guided institutional development, assisted in the allocation of the materials and equipment budget, reviewed and recommended special program/grant requests, and provided input into growth and development of the program as it related to the total college.

The committees consisted of staff representatives from the various divisions/departments and included administrators and, in two colleges, students. This means that each committee member served as a liaison between the learning resources center and the area being represented, thus providing a systematic channel for communications. Only two of the colleges included students as active committee members. The members of the committees were selected in several different ways—in one they are appointed by the president; in three, elected or chosen by their divisions or departments; and in one instance, the member is from the representative assembly's standing committee on the learning resources center. The student representatives were appointed through the student body organization.

From the comments made, it appears that the majority of the members were chosen because of their interest, knowledge, or use of the learning resources program. However, the impact of the advisory committees upon the development of the LRC program had not been very effective. Their major purpose was to advise on policies and issues, to provide a sounding board, and to be a buffer between the learning resources center staff and the college.

The two institutions which did not have advisory committees felt that through individual consultations and relationships with the various departments, the needed input was provided. These two colleges believed that a committee structure often hampers instead of facilitating the flow of communication.

PROCESS FOR INITIATING INNOVATION

The process for initiating innovation in the seven community colleges was rather consistent. Generally, there was no systematic process used in designing instructional change. Each person designed or redesigned his/her course according to perceived needs or desires. The one college which had established a process found that it was not strictly adhered to.

Release time from teaching assignments for instructional development was supposedly available in five colleges. However, on at least three campuses, few cases could be found where release time was granted. Since release time is a necessity if instructional development is to occur in a systematic and effective way, attention must be given to the establishment and implementation of policies and procedures which govern the use of release time.

Three colleges had budgeted monies for developing instructional materials. One college had set aside 1 percent of the college's yearly instructional budget, while another had allotted approximately fifty thousand dollars annually.

The diagram in Figure 6 shows the process by which instructional materials development was initiated using the services of the learning resources program.

It appeared that more and more faculty members were adopting a team approach to instructional development and including staff of the learning resources center. In addition to providing materials and support services, the LRC staff, along with the faculty, were taking an active role in developing instructional programs and in suggesting appropriate strategies for presenting the content to students.

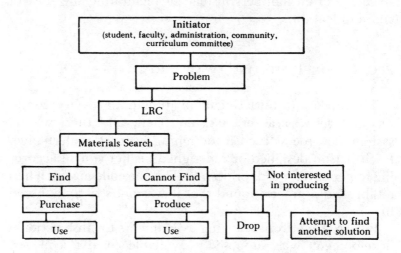

FIGURE 6

INSTRUCTIONAL PROCESS INVOLVING MATERIALS

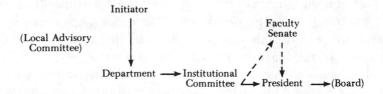

FIGURE 7

There was a review process for innovative changes being initiated on all seven campuses. Once a course had been approved, complete academic freedom was enjoyed by the faculty, thus enabling them to update content and change basic structure without further approval. A composite of the approval procedure for new courses or programs in the seven colleges is shown in Figure 7.

The institutional committees were most concerned with instructional change. Before approving courses, they examined present and future program needs, areas of weakness within existing programs, and community-wide needs. To facilitate this process, a long-range assessment process would be helpful, for it would enable the colleges to monitor developmental activities systematically.

On campuses that do not have a structure for dealing with instructional development, a curriculum design committee might be established. The committee should consist of faculty representatives, a curriculum designer, representatives of appropriate lay citizen groups, possibly student representatives, and materials/production staff from the LRC.

An open atmosphere existed throughout the seven campuses, and staff were encouraged to experiment with new techniques and strategies. Instructional change and improvement was reflected in the materials being selected and used and in services being requested by students and faculty. On one campus, faculty members had asked that a production facility be created for their use. They felt this would assist them in designing innovative instructional changes. The learning resources center was providing excellent services in this area, but the faculty insisted that they must be involved in developing their own teaching materials. These materials could later be refined by the learning resources center staff and added to the center's holdings.

DISSIMILAR RESPONSES

EXISTING PLANNING DOCUMENTS

The planning documents which existed in the seven colleges varied considerably. In addition to differences in content, the process by which the short- and long-range goals and objectives of the learning resources program were developed was quite different. Some of the differences follow:

1. All seven institutions had short-range documents; however, only four had plans which projected activities for three or more years. There was no evidence of any systematic planning on two of the campuses.

2. Four of the seven colleges had sections in overall college documents describing the learning resources program objectives.

3. One college had a district-wide planning program which included management-by-objectives, participatory management, and three-year objectives for the district, each college within the district, and each area of discipline within each college.

4. Five of the seven institutions prepared an extensive annual report presenting a narrative overview of the learning resources program along with statistical substantiation. Two colleges had recently completed self-study reports for regional accreditation visits.

5. Procedure manuals were available in four of the seven institutions, but the contents of these handbooks varied greatly.

6. Two college-wide faculty handbooks contained a section on the LRC's philosophy, services, policies, staff,

and hours. Brochures were available for students and faculty in all seven colleges, ranging from a brief overview to a lengthy document describing the entire learning resources program.

7. Learning resources staff were actively involved in formulating planning documents in five of the seven institutions. The two institutions not having a systematic planning process provided few opportunities for staff input in drafting college-wide goals and objective statements.

DEVELOPMENT OF THE LEARNING RESOURCES CENTER PROGRAM

The development of the learning resources program in each of the seven colleges is a story in itself. Even where common elements were present, each program had developed according to the community college's specific needs.

In three of the colleges, the learning resources program had originated as a unified print and nonprint program. In these three instances, there was from the beginning complete support and commitment to the learning resources center concept from the president and board of trustees. Limited learning resource services had begun in temporary facilities, but once in permanent facilities, the services, functions, and resources had expanded. In one of the three colleges, a library technical assistance program, formed as a department within the learning resources program, had provided a direct and continuous instructional activity for the LRC program.

On another campus, library (print-oriented) services had been established prior to audiovisual services. As equipment began to accumulate, the faculty had put pressure on the college administration to establish a centralized audiovisual services program. The result was the creation of two separate materials service programs. Given the same staff rank, the audiovisual head and the head librarian had both reported to the dean of faculty. Since the audiovisual *materials* were already a part of the library's holdings, the audiovisual person's responsibility was for handling equipment distribution and local production. On the occasion of staff changes, and due to the need for greater coordination, the library and audiovisual center were consolidated to form the division of learning resources with the head librarian named director. Television production was the latest unit to be added to the college's learning resources program.

At the time of the opening of the three remaining community colleges, library services and audiovisual services were separate. However, in two of these, the programs had been unified in the early 1960s. This consolidation made possible an expansion in services and an increase in the number of staff members. Once again, the support of the administration played a major role in the creation of the learning resources program. National trends and concerns expressed by library and audiovisual personnel as well as faculty members were instrumental factors in causing the consolidation of all instructional material into one program area—the learning resources program.

INTERAGENCY COOPERATIVE ACTIVITIES

All seven colleges were involved, in differing degrees, in cooperative activities at the community and state levels. Three of the colleges were heavily involved in cooperative projects which extended beyond their states.

The local public library's microfilm catalog of holdings was being purchased by one institution. This was to assist in preventing unnecessary duplication between the two collections and to aid users in doing bibliographic searches. Another college and public library were collaborating in a consumer information program, using a mobile van. In still another college, there existed cooperative purchasing and processing between the community college and other area libraries.

Three of the colleges were part of a district community college system. In these cases, the various campuses were engaged in cooperative activities among themselves which consisted primarily of loaning resources and program development.

Two institutions made extensive use of local commercial radio. In addition to public relations efforts, they provided courses to area residents. Two colleges were actively involved in sharing television programs with other area colleges.

At the state level, the approach to cooperative activities changed emphasis from direct patron services to informational exchange activities, such as working with associations, consortia, and general program meetings. Six of the seven colleges were involved in activities sponsored by the state library agency. In three instances these involved interlibrary loan networks. In one case the state library had provided assistance in processing materials but had been forced to discontinue the service due to the lack of funds.

Three community colleges were involved in cooperative projects beyond their own state boundaries. These colleges had developed programs which met their own specific needs and then released them for national use. Two colleges had developed television programs which gained nationwide distribution. One of these colleges had produced two 16mm films which were being sold on a commercial basis. The other institution had produced three television series which had been aired as part of two national networks' educational television programming. At the time of the visits, this college was involved in a tri-state middle management television inservice training project.

One college was actively involved in two projects which had brought national recognition to the campus. One project was concerned with the improvement of the learning environment and program opportunities through its membership in the League of Innovation. The second project consisted of three colleges participating in the development and production of learning resources program packages in consumerism, health science, and business education. These three programs were to be added to other existing programs and distributed via a high-speed transmission system. This project, known as ACCESS, (Association of Community Colleges for Excellence in Systems and Services), is the one described in Chapter IV.

LEARNING RESOURCES
ADMINISTRATIVE ORGANIZATION

The administrative organization of the learning resources programs varied considerably. Five of the administrators of the programs reported to an academic dean within the overall college administration. Two heads of learning resources center programs reported to vice-presidents—one of them for academic affairs and the other with college-wide responsibilities. In all seven institutions, the learning resources administrator was a member of the administrative staff, thus providing opportunities for the exchange of program ideas and facilitating communications.

Since there is such variance in the seven organizational patterns, their organizational structure and appropriate accompanying information is provided.* The colleges are identified by the control number assigned to their initial questionnaire.

---

*The reader is reminded that the information presented reflects the organization as it existed at the time of the visit, since in several instances changes have occurred.

Community College 11. The organizational structure of this program separated materials production and use from technical services. This enabled the material utilization consultants to work with the faculty in all stages of instructional development. (See Figure 8 for organizational chart.)

Community College 22. In this college the learning resources program had a written "Charter and Agreement for the Learning Resource Center." Included in the charter is a section which describes the seven areas included in the learning resources center. Each area was headed by a specialist responsible for daily operational decisions, i.e., budget, personnel, and procedures. The following seven areas made up the learning resources center:

1. Audiovisual Services included acquisition, circulation, inventory, and minor maintenance of equipment and nonbook materials, as well as some nonbook instructional materials production for the instructional staff of the college.

2. Electronic Production provided for the development, production, and distribution of audio and video programs relating first to instruction, then to other areas and programs of the college.

3. Instructional Technology provided the following services for the instructional programs of the college: testing and evaluation of media programs and equipment, consultation, proposal writing, and curriculum development.

4. Library Services included acquisitions, cataloging, reference assistance, circulation of book and nonbook materials for curriculum support and for the benefit of students, instructional staff, college administrators,

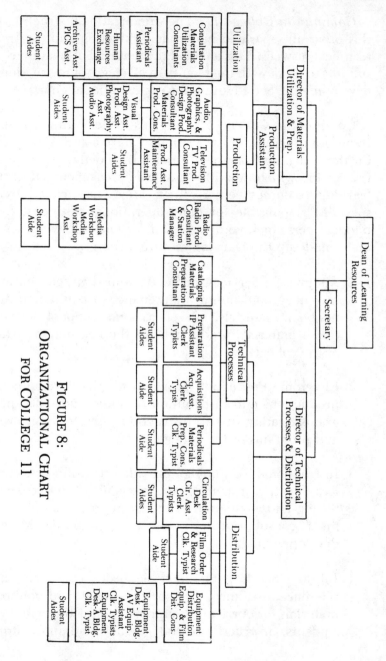

FIGURE 8:
ORGANIZATIONAL CHART
FOR COLLEGE 11

and community patrons.

5. Printing and Graphics Services were designed to meet the following priorities with relation to the printing and/or graphic design of materials: (1) instructional needs, (2) administrative needs, and (3) student and staff needs.

6. Study Skills Learning Center met the instructional needs of a wide variety of special students from developmental through accelerated programs and were specifically designed for each individual.

7. Administrative Section of the learning resources center (1) provided an atmosphere of cooperation and a vehicle for team work, (2) coordinated that team in the solution of instructional and institutional media-related problems, and (3) assured conformity to the policies of the board of education and the college administration. The LRC administration also provided archival services including acquisition, processing, and making the official records of the college available for research.

Community College 81. There were three separate units administered by a person in charge. The heads of these areas worked primarily with faculty and students engaged in instructional activities. (The organizational chart is shown in Figure 9).

Printing services were not part of this learning resources program. The administrator of the program believed that this is more of a service area for the administration and that instructional support services would be secondary. Thus, printing and duplication were provided through another unit within the college.

Community College 109. The learning resources center

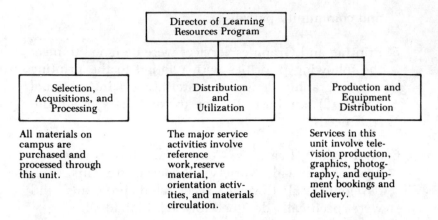

FIGURE 9: ORGANIZATIONAL CHART FOR COLLEGE 81

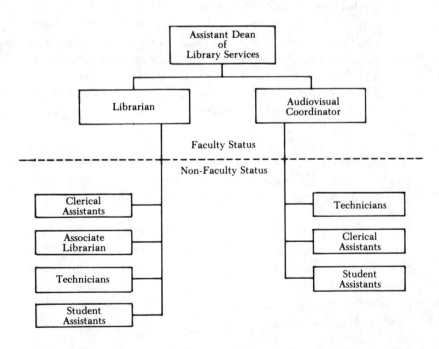

FIGURE 10: ORGANIZATIONAL CHART FOR COLLEGE 109

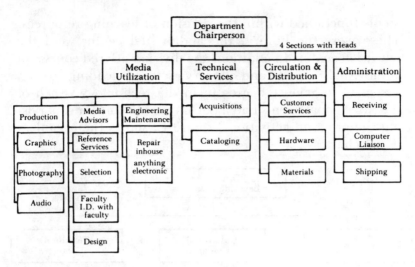

FIGURE 11: ORGANIZATIONAL CHART FOR COLLEGE 118

combines the services of the college library and audiovisual department. There were six departments within the learning resources center: public services, acquisitions and cataloging, computer-assisted learning center, listening center, center for independent learning, and audiovisual/production area. Video taping and television programming were handled by the department of broadcasting. (The organizational chart in figure 10 indicates the staff structure.)

Community College 118. The learning resources program served as an academic support system for the entire college. The head of the media utilization section indicated that if the program is to work, the structure must be simple and permit the staff to provide services as easily and readily as possible. (The organizational chart appears in Figure 11).

Community College 143. In order to maximize service, the policies and structure of the center had been kept as liberal and as minimal as possible. Three service departments functioned within the division of learning resources. These were the library, the audiovisual center, and the television center. In addition, the division offered courses in audiovisual media and library science leading to an Associate in Science degree in media technology. Each of the three departments had a person responsible for supervising the program activities. (Figure 12 shows the organizational chart.)

FIGURE 12: ORGANIZATIONAL CHART FOR COLLEGE 143

A proposal has been made to add computer-assisted instruction to the learning resources program. An instructional media area with carrels and appropriate equipment has been added to the library unit. This was done so that individualized instructional activities could be provided within the center.

Community College 164. The learning resources program was headed by an associate dean for instructional resources. This college was a part of a community college district. At the district level there was a coordinator for instructional resources who provided services—mainly book catalog, centralized ordering, and 16mm film circulation—but had no administrative responsibility. There were three departments within the campus' instructional resources division. Each of these departments was chaired by an individual selected by the departmental staff members. There was no pay differential for serving in this capacity. (The organizational chart for the division of instructional resources is given in Figure 13.)

This chapter has given an overview and documentation of the information gained from visits to seven community college learning resources programs. Since the purpose is to be neither evaluative nor judgmental, the information has been presented without reference to name. The seven provide examples of effective learning resources programs, which are an integral part of the college's instructional process.

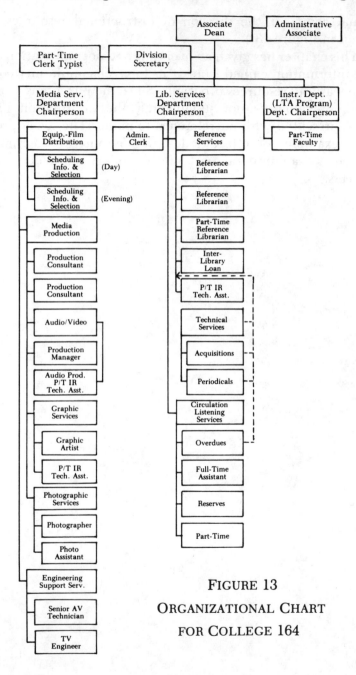

FIGURE 13

ORGANIZATIONAL CHART

FOR COLLEGE 164

Chapter VII
Guideline Statements

The data collected from the initial questionnaires and seven site visits provide the basis for generating the guideline statements. The statements can provide direction for the greater use of learning resources center materials and services within the community college instructional program and are designed to assist planners, designers, and implementers of community college learning resources programs. It is not the intent of these guidelines to outline exact procedures for developing a learning resources program but rather to list the specific factors by which a structure and a climate is created for developing a learning resources program which is truly part of the college's instructional core.

The guidelines are based upon the assumption that learning resources personnel are already providing such services as accessibility of resources, reference or information referral, consultation/planning with faculty and students, and instruction in the use of the learning resources program.

Because of the complexity of the data, a panel of five experts assisted in substantiating the merit of each statement. The panelists were selected on a nationwide basis according to the criteria established. (See Introduction, page 25). The panel members included a community college president, an instructor, and three administrators of learning resources programs.

The guidelines (Appendix I) are divided into five areas:

181

general, personnel, functions, public relations, and instructional development. From the data collected, fifteen major statements and fifty subpoints were written and presented to the five panel members. The panelists were asked to check either the "agree" column, which indicated that they felt that the content of the guideline statement should be heeded by a community college learning resources program, or to check the "disagree" column, which indicated that the service should not be a part of a learning resources program. The panelists were also asked to provide comments which would help in clarifying their responses or provide directions for planners, designers, and implementers of learning resources programs.

The last section of the guidelines presented to the panelists asked them to list additional criteria which were not stated in one of the five areas. Two panelists provided three additional items in these areas:

General. Instructional development and production consultation should be a new statement added to the learning resources support area.

Public Relations. The public (the communities served by the community college) should also be informed. An effective learning resources program meets learning needs of students, instructional needs of faculty, and the continuing education needs of the community.

Instructional Development. At least one member of the professional staff of the learning resources center should have the necessary expertise to assist faculty in the following activities:

1. writing performance or behavioral objectives
2. developing instructional strategies
3. selecting appropriate media (print and nonprint)

to be used with the strategies in achieving the objectives

The reaction of the panelists to each statement is indicated. Those items receiving five favorable responses are indicated by "Unanimous Support"; those receiving four positive responses are indicated by "Favorable Reaction"; and those receiving three or less positive responses are indicated by "In Contention." Comments provided by the five panelists are included below the relevant statement (•) when their remarks add substantially to the clarification of an item.

GENERAL

1. Learning resources should be organized as a single program under the leadership of one director. (UNANIMOUS SUPPORT)
   - Director is a specific title—many people are Assistant Dean, Chairman, etc; use "administrator."
   - This should, however, be an option for each institution. Organizational structure is not as significant as accomplishing the other objectives.

2. All facilities for learning resources, with the possible exception of storage areas, should be located in one building. (IN CONTENTION)

   - Most should, but such facilities as learning laboratories, lecture halls for multi-media presentations, etc., can be, and sometimes should be, elsewhere.
   - An exception might possibly be a TV studio. Also, take into consideration multi-campus operations,

each campus having an LRC which, of course, should be located in one building.
- As the principal component of a campus-wide learning resources program, there should be a well-equipped learning resources center. In addition to that, learning resources, services, and facilities should be decentralized whenever it best serves the needs of students and faculty to do so.

3. Space allocations for the learning resources program should approximate 8,000 square feet for each 1,000 full-time students enrolled. (IN CONTENTION)

- I have no comment on this. I checked "agree" since it seems appropriate. Assume that 8,000 square feet for each 1,000 students includes all space, including storage, production, office, etc., for LRC.
- Space needs to be considered using variables such as instructional modes being used, number of teachers, whether LRC includes learning assistance, etc. Small colleges need more average square feet per student than large colleges.
- I disagree because (1) I have seen no research on this and (2) I suspect that for more complex institutions it may be too low. Certainly it is less than our present space per full-time equivalent (FTE) student (which is overcrowded). Space totals should be related to program as well as to students (for example, is a television production facility needed with more than one studio?).
- I currently have less than 32,000 square feet in which to conduct an integrated library-audiovisual media program for 4,000 full-time equivalent (FTE) students (approximately 8,000 headcount).

This is not adequate for an effective learning resources program. Crowded conditions exist, especially in the media services area of our library media center. An area of 8,000 square feet per 1,000 FTE students might be adequate, if additional space were provided for TV studio functions and for dial-access, cable TV and similar systems.

4. The budget for learning resources should be approximately 5 percent of the total college budget. (IN CONTENTION)

- Here again I think this 5 percent figure may be relative. If you use the 5 percent figure, why not suggest workable alternatives based upon such factors as size, population, kind of instructional strategies, etc.
- Need more because of comprehensive nature of the program; library alone used to be 5 percent. Suggest at least 7–8 percent.
- Assume this includes salaries, capital equipment, and operating expenses.
- Five percent is totally inadequate for a viable, effective, integrated learning resources program. Seven percent should be considered minimal; ten percent or more would be my recommendation. The now outdated 1960 ALA Standards for Junior College Librarians called for five percent of the budget for print materials only—plus an additional amount for AV materials and equipment.

5. The following services represent the core of support provided by learning resources to faculty members:

a. Consultation regarding needed materials and

services (UNANIMOUS SUPPORT)

- Yes, but this guideline should extend to the total program, not just to materials and services.

b. Instruction in using the learning resources program (UNANIMOUS SUPPORT)

c. Preview of materials (UNANIMOUS SUPPORT)

- Equipment and everything else.

d. Ordering new materials on request (UNANIMOUS SUPPORT)

- Do not limit to "on request." The department also has a collection-building responsibility that only the director and his personnel can do. This is also a service to faculty, staff and students.

e. Securing interlibrary loans (UNANIMOUS SUPPORT)

f. Maintaining a "professional collection" for faculty use (FAVORABLE REACTION)

- These materials could be housed in a separate room or area, or they could be integrated into the general print and nonprint collections of the center. The latter approach makes these materials available to more users—both students and faculty.
- In general, educational-topic-related materials should be the responsibility of the instructors.
- As a separate collection, no—having the professional materials in the collection, yes.

   g. Providing closed reserve services (FAVORABLE
      REACTION)

    • Reserve services are usually controlled but not
      closed.

   h. Providing duplicating and printing services to
      support instruction (IN CONTENTION)

    • An optional element which could be provided but
      is not mandatory where alternatives are provided.
    • Depends upon institution and institutional organ-
      ization. This requires considerable discussion.
      Can be a major headache and bone of contention
      for faculty and staff which LRC doesn't need and
      which detracts from basic (core) LRC program.
      On the other hand, can strengthen (give power) to
      LRC.
    • I think they are a natural extension of the learning
      resources center.
   i. Local production services, including production
      staff and budgetary support for innovative in-
      structional materials (UNANIMOUS SUPPORT)
   j. Production of audio and visual experiences in a
      variety of formats (UNANIMOUS SUPPORT)
   k. Providing recordings of **audio** and/or **visual** exper-
      iences as class assignments to be completed in the
      learning resources facilities (UNANIMOUS SUP-
      PORT)

    • What about those activities that are not class
      assignments?
   l. Inservice training in the use of educational media
      (UNANIMOUS SUPPORT)
  m. Providing an evaluation process for measuring the

effectiveness of the services being offered by the learning resources program (UNANIMOUS SUP-PORT)

PERSONNEL

6. Staffing in the learning resources program should be based upon the following:

   a. One professional staff member for each 25 full-time faculty members or 500 full-time students (IN CONTENTION)

   • Quantitative standards, wherever stated, should reflect alternatives.
   • Where added services are provided, additional professionals may be needed beyond this minimum.
   • Many colleges have high ratios of full-time to part-time faculty. This is a ratio that is expanding throughout the country as budgets get tight. What implications for your ratio above?
   • Not possible.
   • Seems O.K.

   b. Approximately one clerical/technical staff member for each professional staff member (IN CONTENTION)

   • Seems O.K.
   • Fiscally impossible and not desirable. At least three to one. Keep professionals doing professional work!
   • There should be a minimum of two clerical/technical (support) staff members for each profes-

sional staff member. A three-to-one ratio is preferred.

c. One part-time student assistant for each 150 students enrolled (IN CONTENTION)

• Somewhat high for larger institution. For example, this would mean 140 for us, about 15 percent above our usable maximum for student positions.
• Part-time could mean from 1 to 15 hours per week—too much of a variable to comment. We use 200 hours per week for 1,600 FTE.

7. The director (principal professional) of the learning resources program should:

a. Be a member of the college administrative team with appropriate rank and title (UNANIMOUS SUPPORT)

• Important to be *above* department or division head status.
• If a member of college administration, individual may not hold rank if college policy dictates, as is case in many community colleges.
• I think it is extremely important for the "principal professional" to be a part of the *top* administrative team in the college (the one that is the major decision-making body). The rank and title of associate dean, or dean of learning resources, might be needed to ensure membership on this important team.

b. Develop the learning resources program annual budget (UNANIMOUS SUPPORT)
c. Report to the dean or vice-president having

college-wide responsibility for academic leadership (FAVORABLE REACTION)

- Guidelines relative to this should be carefully considered. The person reported to may have academic leadership but may not be sympathetic to or conversant with LRC principles. He may not know enough about the total operation to be supportive or take direct action.
- Or directly to the president of the college. The latter is especially important if the "principal professional" is not a member of the top decision-making administrative team of the college.

d. Have a twelve-month contract (FAVORABLE REACTION)

- This may depend upon the organizational pattern of the institution, and I think your guidelines should make note of that. Inter-sessions? Summer sessions? Etc.
- In small schools, eleven months may be sufficient.
- Twelve-month contract is not needed if no summer program and if less than 1,500 FTE students in regular term.

8. The professional staff of the learning resources program should:

a. Have rank, status, and benefits of other college employees (IN CONTENTION)

- Rank, status, and benefits of other faculty and professionals.
- With the exception of the "principal professional" (director, associate dean, or dean of learning

resources), all of the professional staff of the learning resources program should have faculty rank and status.

b. Be assigned to learning resources program operations exclusively (i.e., not hold split assignments with other administrative or instructional duties) (IN CONTENTION)

- While generally I would agree, there are advantages many times from split assignments which should not be ignored. In such assignments, adequate time should be scheduled away from learning resources duties.
- True for administrator, *not* rest of professional staff. I have had many other instructional responsibilities and found this to be a satisfying thing as well as helpful in truly integrating the learning resources program into the total instructional program.
- Conceptually, I agree; however, politically and practically, I don't agree. It depends on the college and the personalities involved, history, geography, funding, union or not, etc.

c. Have assigned time for instructional development assistance to the teaching faculty (FAVORABLE REACTION)

- If, by instructional development, you mean a demonstration of how the LRC can enhance, support, expand instruction, yes.
- This is too important to be left to chance.

d. Serve on curriculum committees to provide liaison to the learning resources program (FAVORABLE

REACTION)

- Very important.
- This committee's function is not design but approval after the design has been developed. If this is true, generally there would be no need for LRC staff to serve on it. LRC staff should be in at the designing stage.

e. Be involved in the development and writing of proposals for off-campus funding (FAVORABLE REACTION)

- Should have input, however. LRC (people) often stuck with supporting grants for oddball projects for which no funds are committed for LRC to help implement the project.
- And, hopefully, working with an experienced grant writer hired by the college for this purpose.

f. Serve as catalyst in encouraging the teaching faculty to use creative and varied instructional methods (UNANIMOUS SUPPORT)

g. Have twelve-month contracts (IN CONTENTION)

- This depends upon organizational pattern of institution.
- Desirable as they are, alternatives should be provided for travel, family, and advanced educational opportunities.
- Except in small colleges.
- Community colleges heavy in year-round teaching/learning.
- If the professional staff (other than the "principal professional") has faculty rank and status, the

regular contract should be for nine months, with
extended contracts offered individual professionals when necessary.

FUNCTIONS

9. The basic functions of the learning resources program
   include:
   a. Serving as a clearinghouse for all college-wide
      purchases of instructional materials and equip-
      ment (FAVORABLE REACTION)

   - Important.
   - ". . .all college-wide purchases of instructional
     materials and equipment"—a strong statement,
     needs modification. Some purchases of instruc-
     tional materials are best left with individual
     departmental budgets.
   - If you mean library books, periodicals,
     audiovisual materials, and audiovisual equip-
     ment. The LRC should maintain an up-to-date
     inventory (including location) of these items.

   b. Coordinating study skill centers or laboratories
      established to assist in student learning activities
      (FAVORABLE REACTION)

10. Some suggested policies of the learning resources pro-
    gram include:
    a. Grouping materials by format and filing them on
       open shelves for easy patron access (IN CONTEN-
       TION)

    - Not necessarily; formats may be mixed according
      to subject, interest, ease of access, etc. Rethink

this one.

- A consistent organization of materials is necessary but not all formats should be on either open or closed shelves, as in the case of reserve books.
- Prefer integrated shelving.
- Grouping materials by format is preferred over grouping materials (print and nonprint) by classification system. Although one can browse among books, some preview or listen to audiovisual materials. Knowing where audiovisual materials are stored is more important than how they are stored. (The catalogs can list the locations.) Some of these materials might best be stored in cabinets or in racks rather than placed or filed on open shelves.

b. Making equipment necessary for proper use of materials accessible for use within the learning resources area and classrooms (UNANIMOUS SUPPORT)

- What about other areas?

c. Opening the learning resources center during all class hours, evenings, weekends, and holidays for use by students, faculty, and area residents who are not enrolled at the community college (IN CONTENTION)

- This guideline should indicate the difficulties inherent in this kind of scheduling.
- Generally the widest numbers of hours open consistent with need is desirable. Certainly a minimum of sixty hours is needed; at all times when there are classes or when usage justifies, the

library should be available.
- First priority is to enrolled students. Then, if funds permit, opening at hours and days mentioned. Should be based on a cost benefit analysis, e.g., the additional cost of openings suggested.
- Need depends upon local circumstances — availability of other library facilities, etc.
- Only if there is enough staff to keep the learning resources center adequately staffed on weekends and during holidays. I feel it is important to have a professional staff member on duty each hour the LRC is open.

PUBLIC RELATIONS

11. The community college adminstration and personnel should be informed of the learning resources center's:

a. Functions (UNANIMOUS SUPPORT)

- "Informed", "aware" suggest little positive action. Reword this guideline so that it reflects definite, strong action.
- LRC director must have as one of his major functions the selling of the LRC to the rest of the college, especially the president and business manager.

b. Services (UNANIMOUS SUPPORT)
c. Programs (UNANIMOUS SUPPORT)
d. Materials (UNANIMOUS SUPPORT)
e. Needs (UNANIMOUS SUPPORT)

- Use faculty to help. Don't embarrass the president or business manager crying all the time to everyone about your needs. Don't use overkill here—be selective. Prioritize needs and then go after through a carefully thought-out public relations campaign.

12. This communication should be accomplished by means of:

a. Annual report (UNANIMOUS SUPPORT)

- Provided other departments prepare them.
- Should be innovative, not a traditional report loaded with statistics; otherwise very few people will read it. May need two versions—short, punchy, easily and quickly read and a lengthy, professional report for immediate boss.

b. Statements of short and long-range goals (UNANIMOUS SUPPORT)
c. Policy statements (UNANIMOUS SUPPORT)
d. Faculty and student handbooks (UNANIMOUS SUPPORT)

- Newsletters.

e. Advisory committee (UNANIMOUS SUPPORT)
f. Reports and office meetings (UNANIMOUS SUPPORT)
g. Bibliographies (UNANIMOUS SUPPORT)
h. Displays (UNANIMOUS SUPPORT)
i. Orientation sessions (UNANIMOUS SUPPORT)
j. Inservice sessions (UNANIMOUS SUPPORT)

13. The learning resources program should be a participating member of existing or future cooperatively established networks which will insure maximum ac-

cessibility and availability of instructional resources and services. (UNANIMOUS SUPPORT)

- Very important.
- Please specify; this may be limited by geographic, demographic, legal aspects, etc.

INSTRUCTIONAL DEVELOPMENT

14. Instructional development should be encouraged by the following:

a. Establishment of teams of individuals possessing different competencies, experiences, and training for the purpose of designing instructional programs (FAVORABLE REACTION)

- Budget-wise this will be a tough one to implement.
- If staff and budget permit.
- This seems to me not to be the responsibility of the LRC staff, but rather a function of the instructional management. LRC can provide support. LRC can establish teams of the individuals on its own staff.

b. Allocation of a certain percentage of the college's budget for instructional development activities (FAVORABLE REACTION)

- Not the usual practice at this time.
- Who provides this? What is the LRC function in its provision?

c. Granting of release time from instructional

teaching assignments to faculty members engaged in major instructional development activities (FAVORABLE REACTION)

- LRC cannot provide this.

d. Provision for personal recognition to faculty and members of the learning resources program (FAVORABLE REACTION)
e. A portion of the teaching faculty evaluation form which relates to the use of media within a classroom setting (IN CONTENTION)

- This negates the whole purpose of the effective use of media as a support to the teaching function.
- Not a 100 percent requirement for 100 percent of the faculty.

f. Establishment on each college campus of a review process for initiating instructional change flexible enough to allow each person to design or redesign programs (FAVORABLE REACTION)

- Are you stating this as a responsibility of the LRC? If so, I strongly disagree.

g. Provision that the teaching faculty have the freedom to develop their own course content and use methods befitting themselves which will meet the college's instructional goals and objectives (UNANIMOUS SUPPORT)

- Insofar as it comes under the aegis of the LRC.
- But consistent with departmental syllabuses and catalogue course descriptions.

- Except that all instructors of the same course should have the same objectives though they may use different methods.

h. Establishment of an inservice program which will assist in training staff in the process and procedures to be used in designing instructional innovation (FAVORABLE REACTION)

- As I see it, designing instructional innovation (whatever that means) is not the true function of the LRC. That function belongs somewhere else in the structure of the college. Once design is accomplished, or during the process, the LRC lends its support, expertise, consultation, etc.

i. Development of a process whereby locally produced/prepared instructional materials are evaluated (UNANIMOUS SUPPORT)

15. Activities which are essential for achieving success in supporting or influencing instruction are:

a. Cooperation between learning resources center staff and the college faculty (UNANIMOUS SUPPORT)
b. Offering a full range of services (UNANIMOUS SUPPORT)

- What is the full range of services?

c. Designing, developing, and producing media (UNANIMOUS SUPPORT)
d. Writing proposals seeking outside funding for use in instructional development activities (IN CON-

TENTION)

- Good, but not essential.
- Only to the extent that the LRC staff is already over burdened if they are doing all the activities mentioned in this study. Ideally, a grants office will assist, LRC will work on it to a degree, and individual faculty members will provide maximum input.
- In these days of restrictive budgets and limited local funding, obtaining outside funding becomes increasingly important if one is to be very effective in furthering instructional development activities and still be able to maintain a dynamic and viable learning resources program.

The above guideline statements provide a context for the development of learning resources programs. The emphasis here is upon the qualitative aspects rather than the quantitative. However, quantities of staff, space, materials, equipment, and funds geared to producing desirable results must be stated in relation to specific institutional goals and objectives. The quality of any learning resources program will ultimately be judged in relation to the successes and failures of the college's instructional program. Each community college will have to translate these statements into a plan which will meet its own goals and objectives.

Chapter VIII
Summary of Findings

Since the founding of the first public community college in 1901, many problems have been studied and examined, but the learning resources programs have not often been addressed specifically. This book aims to provide some basic data on the learning resources program—its services, facilities, staff, organization, and instruction-related activities—and to describe the community college learning resources program in relation to innovative instructional methods.

The data collected in the "Questionnaire on Learning Resources Programs in Relationship to Teaching Innovations in Selected Community Colleges" is reported according to five subdivisions: (1) community college profile, (2) organization and administration of learning resources, (3) arrangement and accessibility of learning resources, (4) instructional services, and (5) instructional development.

After selection criteria were applied to the information collected in the questionnaires, seven community colleges were chosen for site visits. These colleges offered a representative sampling of program components believed to be desirable in order to provide a sound learning resources program. The findings indicate that there are many elements which are essential for inclusion in a learning resources program. However, the organization and arrangement of these elements can be handled in various ways according to the needs of each institution.

Synthesizing the findings from the questionnaires and seven site visits produced a set of guidelines for the development of community college learning resources programs. Because of the complexity of this data and the extensive list of guideline statements, the statements were submitted to a panel of five experts. Their reactions helped to assure that the guideline statements would not be taken out of context nor their meaning misinterpreted by persons in the field.

As indicated in the Introduction, there were nine questions to be examined. The answers to these questions provide a summary for this book.

1. Are print and nonprint services interrelated on community college campuses? If so, how are they related?

   Of the responding 150 community colleges, 122 were providing print and nonprint services from one facility type. The section of the questionnaire pertaining to the arrangement and accessibility of learning resources indicated that faculty and students were receiving print and nonprint services.

2. What proportion of community colleges use media to provide portions of the instructional program for individual learners (learning resources concept)?

   Over 93 percent of the responding 150 community colleges indicated that media were used in providing instruction for individual learners. Learning resources centers comprised 65 percent of the responding colleges, and media centers comprised 16 percent. Only 7 percent of the responding colleges indicated having a central library facility type, where the primary function was to provide print materials.

3. What are the learning resources services provided in those community colleges using the learning resources concept?

More than 75 percent of the learning resources centers provided the following services:

- New print materials ordered on request
- New nonprint materials ordered on request
- Special bibliographies prepared on request
- Print materials placed on closed reserve for specific classes
- Instructor-requested audio disc or tape recordings made available as listening experiences for individuals from specific classes
- Instructor-requested visual materials such as slides, filmstrips, or motion pictures made available as individual viewing assignments for specific classes
- Video tape recordings for individual viewing assignments for specific classes
- Production of copy slides or regular slide sets for use in instruction
- Production of overhead transparencies
- Production of audio recordings in any format (disc, reel-to-reel, cassette)
- Production of video tape recordings
- Provision of services to adapt materials to fulfill the college's instructional program
- Consultation on materials needed in special subject areas
- Consultation on resources needed for units of instruction
- Instruction in the use of the learning resources program
- Guidance in listening and viewing
- Provision of services to adopt materials to fulfill the college's instructional program

4. What are the learning resources facilities in community colleges?

Ninety-three percent of the colleges had permanent

facilities. The learning resources center facility type was administered as one unit in 90 percent of the responding colleges. This facility had an average of almost 30,000 square feet. Two-thirds of the learning resources centers indicated that the total space assigned to learning resources was located in one building. As was observed during the site visits, the centers appeared to be adequate for the number of patrons using the facility in four of the seven colleges.

5. Which of the services provided directly facilitate instruction?

The learning resources program administrators indicated that making materials and equipment readily accessible for faculty use was extremely important in supporting any type of instruction. They agreed that programs should provide an open environment with no barriers placed between the patron and needed resources. The following major services were found to directly facilitate instruction:
- Faculty consultation
- Flexible approach to instructional development
- Community services
- Information retrieval system
- Computer-assisted learning center
- Media production areas
- Career/guidance information projects
- Book catalog
- Integrated media on open shelves
- Resource assistance for nonprint materials in curriculum design
- Audio and video production
- Learning laboratories
- Diversified collection of materials

6. What are the responsibilities of the learning resources staff?

The learning resources staff played an important role in the development and support of the community colleges' educational programs. Staff in most learning resources centers held faculty rank and status. There existed two types of activities by which the learning resources center staff supported and assisted in the development of educational programs:

a. Consultative services were provided through—
- resource acquisitions
- service and program awareness activities with faculty
- programs on equipment and material use
- production services
- previewing services
- instructional development activities
- membership on curriculum committees
- cooperative activities with community groups

b. Direct teaching activities were—
- conducting inservice programs for teaching and administrative personnel
- teaching as a team member in classroom setting
- working with faculty on a one-to-one or small group basis

Seven out of every ten learning resources personnel were not assigned responsibilities outside the learning resources program. Only one out of every five staff was assigned full-time to instructional development. However, three out of every five had part-time instructional development responsibilities.

Three colleges involved in the site visits had full time staff assigned as material utilization specialists or instructional technologists.

7. What are the patterns of administrative organization for community college learning resources services?

The administrative organization of the learning resources programs varied considerably. The administrators of most programs reported to an academic dean or vice-president. The administrator was titled director in more than half of the colleges. Four of the colleges involved in the site visits used the title dean for the chief administrator in the learning resources program. These administrators were members of the administrative staff and held faculty rank and status.

The patterns of organization ranged from a two-division operation with a librarian and an audiovisual coordinator reporting to the dean of library services to an organization whereby seven specialists headed separate areas and were responsible for daily operational activities. These seven areas included audiovisual services, electronic services, library services, instructional technology, printing and graphics, study skill center, and administrative section.. Several colleges expanded the two-division set-up by including a separate division for television instruction program or library technical assistants. Other colleges had separate divisions for circulation and distribution, technical services, or materials production.

8. What are the patterns of development of learning resources programs in community colleges?

The patterns of development of a learning resources program were varied. In the sites visited, three college learning resources programs originated as a unified print and nonprint program. From the beginning there had existed complete support and total commitment to the learning resources center concept from the president and board of trustees.

On one campus, library services were established prior to audiovisual services. As equipment began to accumulate, the audiovisual services program was formed. Eventually the two programs were consolidated into the division of learning resources.

During the early development of the three remaining

community colleges, library services and audiovisual services were formed separately. However, eventually the programs were unified to enable expansion in services and increase in staff size.

Faculty and administrative support, national trends, and concern of library and audiovisual personnel were factors instrumental in causing the consolidation of learning resources.

9. Are there patterns of development, organization, facilities, and services which would optimize future community college learning resources program development?

Throughout this book, the writer has attempted to observe and recognize patterns that help a learning resources center accomplish excellent results and encourage and aid innovative instruction. It can be concluded that there are patterns of development, organization, facilities, and services which optimize the growth of a learning resources program. Descriptive characteristics of these patterns are detailed in chapters V and VI. The concluding guideline statements drawn from these chapters serve as a summation of the promising factors found in the learning resources programs examined in this study.

Several conclusions can be drawn from the above findings:

1. There exists in community colleges a movement toward the combination of print and nonprint materials in one center—a full range of instructionally related activities under the direction of one administrator.

2. The learning resources staff is becoming more involved in the community college teaching team by presenting materials and information in classroom settings.

3. The patterns for developing, administering, and organizing a learning resources program vary considerably.

4. The learning resources program staff is becoming increasingly concerned with community related activities.

5. In a regional examination and comparison of community college learning resources programs, little difference in program characteristics, development, and services could be found.

6. There is a wide variation in the processes by which media innovations for instruction are initiated.

The entire focus has centered around the fact that the community college learning resources program provides a necessary service which is an integral part of the college's instructional program. Both are designed to meet student and faculty needs. Increasingly, the staff of the learning resources program are considered members of the college's instructional team and are providing innovative, diverse, and quality services. Thus, the data collected substantiates the premise that there does exist a relationship between teaching practices and the learning resources program. The information should be of assistance to planners, designers, and implementers of community college learning resources programs.

AFTERWORD

In *O Pioneers!* Willa Cather states "there are only two or three human stories, and they go on repeating themselves as fiercely as if they had never happened before." The persons who have developed community college learning resources programs described throughout this book have contributed to at least one of these human stories. Each program has its own style and methods for achieving its institutional goals, but there are numerous commonalities.

Community college learning resources programs have proven themselves to be an important link in the larger context of information science. They have based their very existence upon their ability to support the colleges' instructional programs. As long as the community college learning resources programs are able to satisfy both of these needs, they will continue to grow and flourish.

As stated throughout this book, it was not my intent to say that any one structure, organization, method, or program was better than another. The only good one is the one which works. The content provides several models or alternatives from which to select, according to individual institutional needs. It is obvious that the learning resources program objectives have helped to determine the college's organization since this program has been involved in college-wide planning.

Community colleges are adaptable to change. Due to their community-based orientation and breakaway from many of the more traditional library and educational approaches, they are able to cast aside what does not work and develop further what does. If any of us are to survive in this field (or any other), we are going to have to respond more quickly and accurately to user needs. Our very survival is dependent upon our capacity to cope with change.

It is services, not words, which have made the community college learning resources program a source and force of educational excellence. The persons staffing these programs have been successful in achieving the five R's:

> Right Material
> > for the
> Right User
> > at the
> Right Place
> > at the
> Right Time to be used
> > in the
> Right Way

This use of media has provided access to necessary information, helping students become engaged in learning activities which address their specific needs. The ability of media to humanize learning and reinforce people-to-people contact has been a success of the learning resources programs.

For learning to occur, students must become personally involved in their educational process. Community colleges have allowed this to happen. The right choice of alternatives is at the very heart of successful education. They have not ignored that it is the student around whom the learning program must be designed.

Community college learning resources programs have not dealt with little plans, for they have stirred, shaped, and changed the instructional process of their parent institutions. The staffs are committed to designing programs which provide a wide range of alternatives which are assisting students engaged in the learning process. They are "a living and breathing thing."

APPENDIXES

APPENDIX A
Definition of Terms

The following definitions are provided for consistency and uniformity:

Audiovisual Center–a unit organized to provide primarily nonprint services and the necessary equipment for proper utilization, which is distributed upon user request.

Central Library–a unit organized to provide primarily information in a print format, organized, stored, and retrieved to fulfill user requests.

Classroom Library–an area maintained in the instructional rooms where materials are shelved without benefit of centralized organization.

Community College–a publicly supported institution of higher education which offers instruction, both formal and informal, below the baccalaureate degree for high school graduates or post–high school age, and provides a program which reflects the specific needs and interests of the local community.

Hardware–the necessary technological devices which are required for the proper use of instructional materials.

Instructional Materials–any artifact or medium used in instruction which enhances the pupil's understanding and/or appreciation.

Instructional Program–the totality of experiences and activities, both planned and unplanned, which has an effect

212

upon the learner in producing some desirable behavioral change related to one or more specific goals.

Instructional Strategy–a way of presenting instructional information and/or conducting instructional activities in
light of an analysis of the teacher, the subject content,
and students.

Learning Resources–printed and nonprinted instructional
materials and the necessary equipment for their proper
use which are an integral part of learning activities and
extend the teaching process by either being auto-
instructional or providing essential units of instruction
for formal coursework.

Learning Resources Center–a unit organized to provide a
full range of instructionally related print and nonprint
services encompassing instructional design and development services which is administered as a single program under the leadership of one director.

Media Center–a unit organized to provide a full range of
print and nonprint materials, necessary equipment,
and services by the staff to fulfill user requests.

Office Library–an area maintained in the individual areas
provided faculty members where materials are shelved
without benefit of centralized organization.

Software–all forms of media which can be used as materials
in the instructional program, as contrasted with hardware.

Teaching Innovation–an idea, practice, activity, application or event which occurs in an instructional situation
which is perceived to be new by an individual or group
of individuals.

Appendix B
Staff Development
Planning Guide

Staff Responsible: _____

Title of Inservice Activity: _____

Purpose: _____
_____
_____
_____
_____

Objectives:

1. _____
_____

2. _____
_____

3. _____
_____

Persons to Be Involved in Planning:

1. _____
2. _____
3. _____
4. _____

Consultants/Persons to Put On Activity:

1. _____
2. _____
3. _____
4. _____

Appendix C
Checklist of Staff Development Planning Activities

Staff Responsible _____
Title of Inservice Activity _____

_____

1. Planning Guide Approval Received _____

2. Program:
   a. Time and Date _____
   b. Place _____
   c. Agenda _____
   d. Printing _____

3. Participants
   a. Audience
      (1) Full-time Faculty _____
      (2) Part-time Faculty _____
      (3) Clerical Staff _____
      (4) Technical Staff _____
      (5) Custodial Staff _____
      (6) Secretaries _____
      (7) Learning Resources Staff _____
      (8) Support Services Staff _____
      (9) Administrators _____
      (10) Board Members _____
      (11) Advisory Committees _____

   b. Announcements to Participants _____

4. Consultants
   a. Justification Written   _____
   b. Selections Made from Human Resource File   _____
   c. Written Exchange of Agreement   _____
   d. Letter of Confirmation   _____
   e. Arrangements:
      (1) Transportation _____
      (2) Hotel _____
      (3) Meals _____
   f. Reimbursement Form _____
   g. Follow-up Letter _____

5. Facilities
   a. Location_____
   b. Equipment
      (1) Microphone _____
      (2) Coffee Pot _____
      (3) Speakers Platform _____
      (4) Audio Equipment (with
          appropriate accessories) _____
      (5) Video Equipment _____
      (6) Extension Cords _____
      (7) Screen _____
   c. Registration Desk _____
   d. Coffee Breaks _____

6. Organization
   a. Preparation of Speeches for Greetings, Opening
      _____
   b. Meal Tickets _____
   c. Identification Tags _____
   d. Packets of Material _____
   e. Name Place Cards_____
   f. Display Materials _____

g. Photographer _____

7. Follow-up
   a. Letters _____
   b. Evaluation_____
   c. Information Dissemination (brochures, reports, pam-
      phlets, etc.) _____

Appendix D
Inservice Evaluation Forms

I.
  A. General (For each question please circle the number on the scale that indicates your opinion.)

  1. How would you rate pre-inservice information and orientation?

1	2	3	4	5
poor		average		excellent

  Comments:

  2. Was the inservice practical in terms of your needs?

1	2	3	4	5
poor		average		excellent

  Comments:

  3. Was the inservice what you expected from the announcement?

1	2	3	4	5
not at all		somewhat		yes

Comments:

4. What is your opinion of the length of time allowed for the inservice?

1	2	3	4	5
too long		about right	not long enough	

Comments:

B. Program (please circle only one answer for each question.)

1. Was the variety of topics/presentations sufficient to maintain your interest?

1	2	3	4	5
poor		average		excellent

Comments:

2. Was the level of the content appropriate?

1	2	3	4	5
too elementary		about right	too advanced	

Comments:

3. Was the quantity of material covered adequate?

1	2	3	4	5
insufficient		about enough	too much	

Comments:

4. Were the sessions with the consultants helpful?

1	2	3	4	5
poor		average		excellent

Comments:

5. Were the objectives of the inservice achieved?

1	2	3	4	5
no		partially		fully

Comments:

C. Results

1. What do you see as the next step(s) for you as a result of this inservice?

2. What would you like for the staff of the learning resources program to do as a follow-up to this inservice?

3. What would you like for the administrators of the college to do as a result of this inservice?

4. Additional comments:

5. Did the inservice fulfill your needs?

1	2	3	4	5
no	somewhat	partially	fully	exceeded my expectations

II. DIRECTIONS: Please circle the number which best represents your reaction to each of the items below:

	Excellent					Poor
1. The organization of the inservice session was:	7	6	5	4	3	2	1

	Clear					Vague
2. The objectives for this inservice session were:	7	6	5	4	3	2	1

	Very Interesting					Dull
3. The treatment of subject matter was:	7	6	5	4	3	2	1

	Very Adequate					Inadequate
4. The quantity of material covered was:	7	6	5	4	3	2	1

	Very Beneficial					No Benefit
5. My participation in this inservice session should prove:	7	6	5	4	3	2	1

	High		Average			Low
6. The presenter (for each item, rate on this continuum:	5	4	3	2	1

_____Was prepared

_____Used a variety of teaching methods

_____Knew subject matter

_____Provided an environment which was conducive to learning

	Excellent					Poor
7. Overall, I consider this inservice to have been:	7	6	5	4	3	2	1

8. Do you feel a need for additional inservice on this topic?   1. Yes   2. No

9. If this session were to be repeated, would you recom-

mend it to others?   1. Yes   2. No
10. Please comment below
on any aspect of this inservice session:
11. List needs for future inservice sessions:

Appendix E
Staff Development Offerings

In the fall of 1976, the League for Innovation in the Community College initiated a project on staff development activities occurring in member colleges. The results were released in the *Staff Development Resource Inventory & Directory 1977*. The following is a listing of those activities which directly relate to or reflect the use of the learning resources program.

A. Teaching and Learning Strategies

　1. Individualized Instruction—Consumnes River College
　　A systematic approach to individualized instruction was the title of an inservice course offered Monday, Wednesday, and Friday during the college's intersession, January 10–28, 1977. The college's instructional media specialist covered problems in instructional development and the use and development of instructional media with hands-on experience.
　　Contact:　Barbara Hoffmann
　　　　　　　Instructional Media Specialist
　　　　　　　Cosumnes River College
　　　　　　　8401 Center Parkway
　　　　　　　Sacramento, California 95823

　2. A Smorgasbord Approach to Individualized Instruc-

tion—Central Piedmont Community College

In response to a request for a workshop on individual-ized instruction for our fall conference, a self-paced, self-prescribed workshop was devised which could be conducted by one staff person and utilized by both faculty experienced in individualized instruction and those who were novices. A variety of print and non-print resources were used, each organized into one of seven categories. The format utilized both independent study and small group work. Each participant received an annotated handout to guide his/her selection of ac-tivities. By converting an office into a "theater" and utilizing dial access carrels, a number of activities were available in a small, concentrated space. A sample page of the handout is available at no cost.

Contact: Mimi Vollum
            Central Piedmont Community College
            P.O. Box 4009
            Charlotte, North Carolina 28204

3. Modular Instruction Workshop Series—Los Angeles Harbor College

   Harbor College has held three workshops and a fourth is planned on the subject of modular instruction. The content of the first two was devoted to "Design and Development" of instructional modules. Following the first workshop, faculty decided on a format for writing modules and some faculty began writing. Software, books, and pamphlets to support the modules were purchased. Five months later the second workshop "Exploring Progress and Problems," was held. The third workshop, one year after the first, centered on "Implementation of Modular instruction." All par-ticipants were encouraged to share their problems, frustrations, and successes in many aspects of im-plementation. Several seminars were held before the series concluded with "Evaluation of Instructional Modules." Following this last workshop, modules which were written were evaluated. Faculty evaluated their own and served on committees of three each to evaluate modules written by other faculty.

Contact: Mary Stanley
           Nursing Learning Laboratory
           Los Angeles Harbor College
           1111 Figueroa Place
           Wilmington, California 90744

4. Alternatives for Learning, Workshop for Certified Staff—Orange Coast College

This is a course granting two units of credit on the salary schedule and dealing with individualization of the learning process. The course meets thirteen times, and participants develop two individualized units and a model for a more extensive individualization of their courseware. Several models of individualization currently in vogue are discussed, and faculty members are allowed to select the one with which they feel the most comfortable. Among those models are the Postlethwait audio-tutorial, the Johnson and Johnson materials, and the Deterline Cistrain materials.

The topic outline includes institutional development (instructional and professional), goals and objectives, models of individualized instruction, programmed instruction with and without the computer, systematic design of curriculum, learning theory for individualized instruction, tracking systems, test construction, selection of media, production of software, evaluation of systems, learners' styles analysis, and the team approach to individualization and major project management.

The purpose of this workshop is to provide an alternative teaching method which is learner-centered for our faculty, and to permit faculty members to experience the techniques before they consider the possibility of redesigning entire courses on an individualized model.

Various materials have been used, some of which are in the public domain, some not. One copy of any public domain item is available to a League college.

Contact: Jeffrey M. Dimsdale
             Instructional Development Specialist
             Orange Coast College
             2701 Faireview Road
             Costa Mesa, California 92626

B. Media

1. IMC Mini-Workshops—Los Angeles Harbor College

The Instructional Media Center offered a series of four workshops to encourage the use of media by interested evening faculty through training in operation of audiovisual equipment and information about media production services, and to acquaint faculty with the IMC staff so they would be able to direct their questions to the appropriate professional.

A series of four workshops was given in a staff lounge on campus between 6 and 9 p.m. Evening instructors were encouraged to drop by during their breaks to gain information from the IMC librarian, electronics technician, instructional media production technician, and IMC clerk. Four different stations, each manned by one of these IMC staff members, dealt with media production services, training in operation of projectors, tape recorders, and VTR equipment, selection of films, and equipment and film booking.

Contact: Pam Bleich
             Instructional Media Center
             Los Angeles Harbor College

1111 Figueroa Place
Wilmington, California 90744

2. A Workshop on Selection and Use of Media—Central Piedmont Community College
A five-hour workshop was designed for a department faculty of approximately fifteen persons to acquaint them with a variety of media and increase their knowledge of proper selection and use of media. No attempt was made to teach operation of hardware; emphasis was on selection and effective use for instructional situations. Small groups rotated through four activity areas, each focused on specific types of media. This was followed by small group work and hypothetical case studies, group sharing, and viewing of a filmstrip on the use of 16mm films. The latter also served as a vehicle for teaching evaluation of audiovisual material. Outline of workship, sample case study, and example of handouts used are available at no cost.
Contact: Mimi Vollum
Central Piedmont Community College
P.O. Box 4009
Charlotte, North Carolina 28204

3. Media Laboratory—Orange Coast College
A "do-it-yourself" media production facility is provided to OCC faculty for the purpose of producing audio materials, slide and overhead transparency production, and experimentation with media not yet available elsewhere on campus. Consultation with a media specialist is available, and the instructor learns how to bypass the inevitable delays of relying on someone else to provide these services. The lab is also used for laboratory activities of the inservice media courses and workshops.
Contact: Donald Rueter

Media Specialist
Orange Coast College
2701 Fairview Road
Costa Mesa, California 92626

4. Television Workshop—Sacramento City College
Several instructors were funded by the staff development committee to produce video tapes during a 1976
summer workshop. The primary objectives of the
workshop were to train instructors in the utilization of
this medium and to develop video tapes that would
enhance the instructional program. A list of video tape
titles produced by this workshop is available.
Contact: John Bucknell
Audiovisual Officer
Sacramento City College
3835 Freeport Boulevard
Sacramento, California 95822

5. Workshops for Part-Time Instructors—Richland College
Richland College offers a series of instructional aids
workshops for part-time instructors, through the
Learning Resources Center. Sessions include:

a. Teaching with the 16mm Film
b. Teaching with the Overhead Projector
c. Audio/slide Production for Fun and Instruction
d. Incorporating Use of Library Materials and
   Reference Books into Research Paper Assignments
e. Using a video Tape Recorder in Teaching
Contact: Dick Smith
Associate Dean for Instructional Services
Richland College
12800 Abrams Road
Dallas, Texas 75243

6. Audiovisual Materials Evaluation Form—Central
Piedmont Community College
A one-page evaluation form was developed for all
faculty and staff to complete when they have ordered
any audiovisual material for possible purchase or for
rental. A five-point evaluation scale is used. In addition,
the reviewer answers brief questions as to potential, extended use, by whom and what type of instructional setting (independent study, classroom, etc.). The form
serves two purposes: (1) it provides data for wiser purchasing decisions and (2) it serves as a subtle training
tool to sharpen faculty's awareness of features which
should be evaluated in audiovisual materials.
A copy of the form is available at no cost.
Contact: Mimi Vollum
           Central Piedmont Community College
           P.O. Box 4009
           Charlotte, North Carolina 28204

7. A Checklist for Evaluating A Self-Instructional Program—Central Piedmont Community College
A simple one-page checklist was devised to assist faculty in evaluating self-instructional materials they were
considering for classroom use, whether commercially
produced or developed by another college. The
checklist directs the reviewer's attention to specific
features, quality indicators, and cost considerations.
A copy of the form is available at no cost.
Contact: Mimi Vollum
           Central Piedmont Community College
           P.O. Box 4009
           Charlotte, North Carolina 28204

8. Staff Film Festival—Richland College
In January 1975 a unique experience in staff development unfolded when eleven films were scheduled for

faculty and staff. No other programming was created. The films covered a variety of topics and ranged in length from nine minutes (*Frank Film* pointing out the present object orientation in society) to 108 minutes (*Wednesday's Child*).

Contact: Linda Catlin
           Administrative Assistant to the President
           Richland College
           12800 Abrams Road
           Dallas, Texas 75243

C. Supportive Activities for Staff Development

1. Community Education Staff Development—Delta College

   Community Education serves the needs of the community which are not met by two-year degrees or academic certificate programs. Community Education includes programs for self-development, individual groups, community development, and goals of organizations and groups. Opportunities are primarily designed for adults and offer learning experiences more conducive to adult learning than conventional methods. The main focus in the Community Education Staff Development plan is to provide a mechanism for articulation between administrative staff responsibilities and instructional commitments. A workshop-seminar program has been implemented to develop skills in the following areas:

   a. Goal statements
   b. Formation and writing of course objectives
   c. Use of media
   d. Evaluative methods—program accountability

   Contact: Karl DuBois
              Dean, Community Affairs
              Delta College

University Center, Michigan 48710

2. "Media Memo"—Cosumnes River College
CRC has found the "Media Memo" to be an invaluable
method of communicating with the faculty and staff of
the college. Graphically attractive (yet economical by
using both sides of the paper) the *Media Memo* informs
faculty about:
  a. Films on campus—those for preview and those
     that have been selected for purchase,
  b. Weekly educational television programming,
  c. New book acquisitions,
  d. New media packages,
  e. TV schedule for open air TV classes, and
  f. League and program and staff development proj-
     ects.
A sample copy is available.
Contact: Terry Kastanis
           Director of Learning Resources
           Cosumnes River College
           8401 Center Parkway
           Sacramento, California 95823

3. Professional Library—Los Angeles Harbor College
Los Angeles Harbor College has developed an on-going
collection of materials pertinent to professional expertise in community college administration and teaching.
This library includes the ERIC microfiche collection
for the community college; a compendium of works by
authorities in the field of community college education; and books, journals, and magazines which relate
to the field as recommended by campus staff.
These works are available to the staff through an honor
checkout system; staff are periodically notified of new
additions to the collection. It is felt that having a
library of professional materials in one location en-

courages easy access and, therefore, exposure to new
and innovative ideas, which we hope will then be applied in instructors' teaching and in more effective
management.

Contact: Sally Gay
            College Development
            Los Angeles Harbor College
            1111 Figueroa Place
            Wilmington, California 90744

4. The Case of the Wayward Worm—Cosumnes River
College
Although written specifically for the Learning
Resource Center at Cosumnes River College, a twenty-
minute video tape entitled "The Case of the Wayward
Worm" is available for loan to members of the League.
Mr. History Instructor wants to visualize and vitalize
his lecture, and in the process he is introduced to the
many services of the Learning Resource Center, i.e.,
graphics, film, commercially prepared media packages, reference/reserve services. Finally, he produces
some of his own materials as well as makes use of those
already available.

The video tape is available for free loan.

Contact: Terry Kastanis
            Director of Learning Resources
            Cosumnes River College
            8401 Center Parkway
            Sacramento, California 95823

5. New Faculty Orientation Course—Orange Coast College
A number of activities designed to orient new members
of the OCC faculty to services available to them is
presented in initial sessions at the beginning of the term
and outlined in detail in a syllabus. The new instructor

contacts and meets various staff members who provide information about particular services and associated facilities, as well as providing guidance in performing activities.

Facilities/programs include instructional TV production, automated test scoring, AV equipment operation and checkout services, library services, etc. Completion of all activities entitles the new instructor to one unit of salary advancement credit.

Contact: Leo LaJeunesse, Director
Media Resources Center
Orange Coast College
2701 Fairview Road
Costa Mesa, California 92626

Appendix F
Questionnaire on Learning Resources Programs in Relationship to Teaching Innovations in Selected Community Colleges

INSTRUCTIONS

1. Please read the entire questionnaire before starting to fill it.out. Doing so will save you time and effort.
2. Appropriate members of the learning resources staff and instructional staff should be involved in completing the questionnaire.
3. In all cases, data and information should be supplied for the 1973–1974 school year.
4. In every instance, please base your responses on information which reflects the elements as found in your program. The intent of this study is not to compare one community college against another.
5. Please return the completed questionnaire by *March 1, 1975.*

COMMUNITY COLLEGE PROFILE

1. Name and address of community college:

   _____

   _____

   _____

2. Name and title of person completing this questionnaire:

   _____

   _____

4. Current number of faculty members employed in this
   community college:
   _____ Full-time
   _____ Part-time

5. This college is currently housed:
   _____Completely on a permanent, separate campus
   _____ Partially on a temporary campus
   _____ Completely on a temporary campus

6. This college location would be best described as:
   _____Central metropolitan   _____Rural
   _____Suburban   _____Other
                                      (specify)

ORGANIZATION AND ADMINISTRATION OF LEARNING
RESOURCES

(Learning resources as used in this questionnaire include all
media used in any one of the six facilities described in question seven.)
   7. Please read the following descriptions and check the
      description which best fits your own situation:
      _____ 1. *Learning Resources Center*: A unit organ-
                 ized to provide a full range of instructional-
                 ly related print and nonprint services en-
                 compassing instructional design and
                 development services administered as a
                 single program under the leadership of one
                 director.
      _____ 2. *Media Center*: A unit organized to provide a

full range of print and nonprint materials, necessary equipment, and services from the media staff to fulfill user requests.

_____ 3. *Central Library*: A unit organized to provide primarily information in a print format, organized, stored, and retrieved to fulfill user requests.

_____ 4. *Audiovisual Center*: A unit organized to provide primarily nonprint services and the necessary equipment for proper utilization and distributed upon user request.

_____ 5. *Classroom Library*: An area maintained in the instructional rooms where materials are shelved without benefit of centralized organization.

_____ 6. *Office Library*: An area maintained in the individual areas provided faculty members where materials are shelved without benefit of centralized organization.

_____ 7. Other (specify):

8. The learning resources on this campus are:

_____ Administered as one unit

_____ Administered as two or more units

9. What is the percentage of the total college budget allocated to learning resources for all purposes?

_____ % of the total college budget

10. What is the approximate square footage occupied by learning resources for all purposes?

_____ total square feet

11. Is the total space assigned to learning resources located in one building?

_____ Yes

_____ No

12. The number of paid professional personnel working in the learning resources program:
   _____ Full-time personnel
   _____ Part-time personnel

13. Most of the professional staff are on contracts for:
   _____ 9 months   _____ 11 months
   _____ 10 months   _____ 12 months

14. The title of the principal learning resources staff member who is responsible for all the service is: _____
   _____

15. To whom in the community college administration does the principal learning resources staff member report?
   _____ 1. President
   _____ 2. Vice-president (with overall campus responsibility)
   _____ 3. Vice-president (with specific responsibility). Please indicate area of responsibility: _____
   _____ 4. Academic dean
   _____ 5. Other (specify): _____

16. The contract for the principal learning resources staff member is:
   _____ 9 months   _____ 11 months
   _____ 10 months   _____ 12 months

17. The number of paid support personnel, not including professional staff is:

	Full-time	Part-time
Aides	_____	_____
Clerks	_____	_____
Technicians	_____	_____

Students (not
indicated above)   _____   _____
Other   _____   _____

18. Are any key learning resources personnel assigned additional responsibilities not related to the operation of the learning resources program? (e.g., instructional load, management of book store)

    _____ Yes (Please describe additional assignments:

    _____

    _____

    _____ No

19. How many professional staff members in the learning resources program have faculty rank and status?

    _____ (number having faculty rank and status)

20. How many professional staff members in the learning resources program are assigned to instructional development work with faculty members?

    _____ Part-time assignment on instructional development activities

    _____ Full-time assignment on instructional development activities

21. How many regular staff members, not in professional classifications, are assigned to instructional development work with faculty members?

    _____ Non-professional staff on part-time instructional development

    _____ Non-professional staff on full-time instructional development

22. Is the principal learning resources staff member responsible for the development of the learning resources program's annual budget?

_____ Yes

_____ No (If no, who is responsible for developing the budget?)_____

23. Which of the following apply to the hours learning resources are available for use by your patrons? (More than one may apply.)

_____ Available during class hours

_____ Available for evening and weekend use during times classes are not being held

_____ Available during vacation and holiday periods

Arrangement and Accessibility of Learning Resources

24. Materials are grouped by format and are filed on open shelves.

_____ Yes   _____ No

25. Materials, regardless of format, are interfiled on open shelves.

_____ Yes   _____ No

26. All materials are made easily accessible for use.

_____ Yes

_____ No (If No, please explain): _____

_____

27. Equipment for proper utilization of materials is made accessible for use within the learning resources areas.

_____ Yes   _____ No

28. Equipment for proper utilization of materials is made accessible for classroom use.

_____ Yes   _____ No

29. Preview of materials is provided.

_____ Yes　　　　_____ No

30. Interlibrary loans will be arranged:
_____ Yes _____ No (For faculty members)
_____ Yes _____ No (For students)

31. The community college personnel are informed of learning resources programs and materials through:
_____ Bibliographies
_____ Conferences
_____ Displays
_____ Exhibits
_____ Orientation sessions
_____ Reports
_____ Inservice sessions
_____ Office meetings
_____ Other (specify): _____

32. The community college administration is informed of the needs of the learning resources program through:
_____ Reports
_____ Office meetings
_____ Other (specify): _____

33. The staff of learning resources is continually reevaluating the collection in terms of:
_____ Changing curriculum content
_____ New teaching techniques
_____ Newer materials available
_____ Other (specify): _____

34. A faculty handbook is available which fully describes all facets of the learning resources program.
_____ Yes　　　　_____ No

35. A student handbook is available which fully describes

all facets of the learning resources program.

_____ Yes   _____ No

36. Are policy statements governing the operation of the learning resources program readily available for faculty, student, and administrator use?

_____ Yes   _____ No

37. The community college staff is informed of new acquisitions through:

_____ Bulletins

_____ Releases in campus newspaper

_____ Displays

_____ Materials sent to departmental offices for examination

_____ Copy of catalog card or book catalog is sent to departmental offices of faculty members.

38. The learning resources program serves as a clearinghouse for all requests for new materials.

_____ Yes   _____ No

39. The learning resources program serves as a clearinghouse for all requests for new equipment.

_____ Yes   _____ No

40. A professional collection of materials is made available for faculty use.

_____ Yes   _____ No

41. The staff of the learning resources program participates as a member of the teaching team by presenting materials and information in classroom settings.

_____ Yes   _____ No

42. The staff of the learning resources program is involved

in cooperative activities with other community groups
and organizations through:

_____ Conferences
_____ Visits
_____ Reports
_____ Bibliographies
_____ Program exchange
_____ Other (specify): _____

43. Staff of the learning resources program serve on curriculum committees.

_____ Yes   _____ No

44. Planning with faculty members keeps the staff of the
learning resources program informed of future
assignments and needs.

_____ Yes   _____ No

45. To what extent is the staff of the learning resources
program involved in planning curricular changes and
teaching/learning innovations?

_____ Slightly (less than 10 involvements per learning resources staff per year)
_____ Moderately (from 11 to 20 involvements per
learning resources staff per year)
_____ Heavily (over 21 involvements per learning
resources staff per year)

Instructional Services:
Please check your judgment on the amount of services
listed below which you offer direct instructional support.

INSTRUCTIONAL SERVICES

SERVICES	FACULTY USE OF THE SERVICE IS GENERALLY				DEPARTMENTAL USE OF THE SERVICE IS GENERALLY							
	Not Provided	Provided to any faculty member	Provided to department	Nonexistent	Light	Medium	Heavy	Nonexistent	Light	Medium	Heavy	
46. New print materials orded on request												
47. New nonprint materials ordered on request												
48. Special bibliographies prepared on request												
49. Print materials placed on closed reserve for specific classes												
50. Instructor request audio disc or tape recordings made available as listening experiences for individuals from specific classes												
51. Instructor request that visual materials such as slides, filmstrips, or motion pictures made available as individual viewing assignments for specific classes												
52. Video tape recordings for individual viewing assignments for specific classes												
53. Production of copy slides or regular slide sets for use in instruction												
54. Production of overhead transparencies												
55. production of audio recordings in any format (disc, reel-to-reel, cassette, and so forth)												
56. Production of video tape recordings												
57. Production of computer-assisted instruction programs												
58. Guidance in listening/viewing is provided												
59. Production of learning packages												
60. Observe students in the center for purposes of sharing with faculty information about interests, needs, and habits of study and reading behavior												
61. Provide program whereby instructional materials and methods can be evaluated according to their teaching effectiveness												
62. Provide a listing of community resources which supports the college's instructional program												
63. Provide services whereby materials can be adopted to fill the college's instructional program												
64. Provide services whereby materials can be adapted to fill the college's instructional program												
65. Consultation on materials needed in special subject areas is provided												
66. Consultation on resources needed for units of instruction is provided												
67. Instruction in the use of the learning resources program is provided												

Instructional Development

68. The staff of the learning resources program works with faculty members in assisting them with the integration of instructional resources into the teaching-learning process.

_____ Yes (If your answer is yes, please complete the following.)

_____ No (If your answer is no, please go to question 69.

_____ Assistance is given under priorities determined in advance.

_____ Assistance is given on a first-come-first-served basis.

_____ Assistance is given to departments or units only, not to individual faculty members.

_____ Assistance is given to individual faculty members as well as departments and units.

_____ Assistance is given according to the number of students to be served.

_____ Assistance is given first to required courses as opposed to elective courses.

_____ Assistance is given only to those faculty members or units willing to share the cost.

_____ Assistance is charged to the individual or instructional unit on a cost basis.

_____ Assistance is not charged to the individual or instructional unit since the budget of the learning resources program is sufficient to cover all costs.

_____ Assistance is given in the production and use of materials which will be used outside the learning resources program facilities.

_____ Assistance is provided faculty members in all phases of producing learning packages.

(If additional space should be needed in answering the following, please use additional sheets of paper.)

69. In your judgment, what are the specific departments or courses on which your learning resources program has had the greatest effect directly on instruction?

Departments or Instructional Units:	Specific Course Numbers and Titles:
_____	_____
_____	_____
_____	_____
_____	_____

70. What do you consider your greatest success in supporting or influencing instruction?

_____

_____

_____

71. What are major difficulties in supporting or influencing instruction?

_____

_____

_____

Thank you for completing this questionnaire. Please place it in the stamped envelope and return it to me by *March 1, 1975.*

APPENDIX G

Services	Not Provided	Provided to any faculty member	Provided to department	Nonexistent	Light	Medium	Heavy	Nonexistent	Light	Medium	Heavy
	FACULTY USE OF THE SERVICE IS GENERALLY							DEPARTMENTAL USE OF THE SERVICE IS GENERALLY			
New print materials ordered on request	7	135	36	0	12	79	45	3	23	54	28
New nonprint materials ordered on request	5	121	50	0	22	62	46	3	22	57	25
Special bibliographies prepared on request	15	116	29	8	74	37	7	18	51	23	6
Print materials placed on closed reserve for specific classes	9	133	31	1	19	63	50	11	23	30	30
Instructor request audio disc or tape recordings made available as listening experiences for individuals from specific classes	4	140	33	1	27	64	46	8	20	43	23
Instructor request that visual materials such as slides, filmstrips, or motion pictures made available as individual viewing assignments for specific classes	5	139	31	1	30	52	56	9	23	31	30
Video tape recordings for individual viewing assignments for specific classes	21	121	34	4	47	57	19	8	35	36	8
Production of copy slides or regular slide sets for use in instruction	19	125	30	4	33	47	45	10	31	29	19
Production of overhead transparencies	16	119	31	5	43	36	39	9	37	20	19
Production of audio recordings in any format (disc, reel-to-reel, cassette, and so forth)	7	137	34	3	31	51	53	8	25	36	29
Production of video tape recordings	20	119	36	5	57	41	21	10	38	25	11
Production of computer-assisted instruction programs	125	18	7	42	16	2	3	36	8	4	2
Guidance in listening/viewing is provided	26	110	31	8	51	37	15	12	36	24	9
Production of learning packages	39	99	31	15	56	30	8	21	36	20	4
Observe students in the center for purposes of sharing with faculty information about interests, needs, and habits of study and reading behavior	84	53	16	35	38	19	1	29	25	9	0
Provide program whereby instructional materials and methods can be evaluated according to their teaching effectiveness	81	60	20	28	37	19	1	23	25	12	3
Provide a listing of community resources which supports the college's instructional program	93	47	18	32	60	13	4	28	22	6	4
Provide services whereby materials can be adopted to fill the college's instructional program	26	108	41	7	49	47	15	12	34	29	13
Provide services whereby materials can be adapted to fill the college's instructional program	18	113	39	5	61	38	9	12	37	32	7
Consultation on materials needed in special subject areas is provided	2	139	39	1	52	66	16	8	36	42	14
Consultation on resources needed for units of instruction is provided	7	134	39	2	61	59	10	7	46	32	10
Instruction in the use of the learning resources program is provided	5	139	45	1	48	73	17	8	38	40	13

246

APPENDIX H
Site Visit Interview Guide

Name of Community College   Date of Visit

Learning Resources Staff

1. What type of planning documents exist in this community college which illustrate the short-range, long-range goals and objectives of the learning resources program?
2. What is the role that the staff of the learning resources program plays in the educational program?
3. What is the relationship of the learning resources program to innovative instructional programs?
4. Of all the services provided by the learning resources center staff, which are directly related to innovative instruction?
5. What were the processes through which the learning resources center program developed within this community college?
6. What is the nature and extent of faculty involvement in the learning resources center program.
7. What is the learning resources administrative organization in this community college?
8. Is there a committee which serves in an advisory capacity to the learning resources center staff?

_____ Yes   _____ No

If there is, how was it selected and what is its function?

9. What procedures are used for the continuous evaluation of the services being provided by the staff of the
learning resources program?

10. In your opinion, has the proportion of faculty in your
community college using mediated instruction over the
past three years

_____ increased?

_____ decreased?

_____ remained the same?

11. In your opinion, will the proportion of faculty in your
community college be using mediated instruction over
the next three years?

Will it _____ increase? _____ remain the same?
or _____ decrease?

12. What technological systems are being used in this community college?

a. Computer-assisted Instruction

b. Data Processing (Instruction/Administrative)

c. Dial Access

13. What are the characteristics of the learning resources
staff?

a. Education:

b. Experience:

c. Age:

14. What types of interagency cooperative activities are
being provided by the learning resources center program?

Faculty

15. What is the role that the instructional staff plays in the
development of the learning resources program?

16. What innovative teaching practices are currently being
used or are being considered for use in the college's instructional program?

17. What is the process for initiating innovation in this

community college?

Students

18. How often do you use the learning resources program for class related assignments?

_____ Daily _____ Weekly _____ Monthly

19. When you need to use the learning resources program, are you able to find the information you need?

Daily ____Never ____Seldom ____Frequent ____Always

Weekly ____Never ____Seldom ____Frequent ____Always

Monthly ____Never ____Seldom ____Frequent ____Always

APPENDIX I
Learning Resources
Program Guidelines

Introduction

The community college learning resources program should have basic resources which support the institution's purposes and programs. Such resources should be available in a well-equipped facility which encourages maximum use by the campus community. A competent professional staff should be available to assist in the use of resources. The collection of print and nonprint materials should be organized for easy access and adequate hours of service should be maintained.

As used throughout this study, learning resources are defined as printed and nonprinted forms of recorded information and the necessary equipment for their proper utilization. A learning resources center is a unit organized to provide a full range of instructionally related print and nonprint service encompassing instructional design and development services and administered as a single program under the leadership of one director. The community college is a publicly supported institution of higher education offering instruction, both formal and informal, below the baccalaureate degree for persons who are either high school graduates or post–high school age, and providing a program which reflects the specific needs and interests of the local community.

The purpose of these guidelines is to assist planners,

designers, and implementers of community college learning resource programs. The guidelines were based upon information collected through the preliminary questionnaire and site visits.

Directions

1. Listed below are statements which describe elements which might be found in a community college learning resources program.
2. Following each statement appear two columns—agree and disagree. If you believe that the statement should be a part of the learning resources program, place a check in the agree column. If you feel it should not be a part of the learning resources program, place a check in the disagree column.
3. Use the comment space to explain or qualify any of your responses which you believe need explanation.
4. All responses will be treated confidentially. The study will not identify any person or college with any statements being reported.

GUIDELINES

RESPONSES

A. *General*   *Agree   Disagree*

1. Learning resources should be organized as a single program under the leadership of one director.

-----   -----

Comments:

2. All facilities for learning resources, with the possible exception of storage areas, should be located in one building.

_____ _____

Comments:

3. Space allocations for the learning resources program should approximate 8,000 square feet for each 1,000 full-time students enrolled.

_____ _____

Comments:

4. The budget for learning resources should be approximately 5 percent of the total college budget.

_____ _____

Comments:

5. The following services should represent the core of support provided by learning resources to faculty members:
a. Consultation regarding needed materials and services

Comments:

b. Instruction in using the learning resources program

                                                 _____   _____

Comments:

c. Preview of materials

                                               _____   _____
Comments:

d. Ordering new materials on request

                                               _____   _____

Comments:

e. Securing interlibrary loans

                                               _____   _____

Comments:

f. Maintaining a "professional collection" for faculty use

_____   _____

Comments:

g. Providing closed reserve services

_____   _____

Comments:

h. Providing duplicating and printing services to support instruction

_____   _____

Comments:

i. Local production services, including production staff and budgetary support for innovative instructional materials

_____   _____

Comments:

j. Production of audio and video experiences in a variety of formats

                                         _____   _____

Comments:

k. Providing recordings of audio and/or video experiences as class assignments to be completed in the learning resources facilities

                                         _____   _____

Comments:

l. Inservice training in the use of educational media

                                         _____   _____

Comments:

m. Providing an evaluation process for measuring the effectiveness of the services being offered by the learning resources program

                                         _____   _____

Comments:

B.*Personnel*

6. Staffing in the learning resources program should be based upon the following:
   a. One professional staff member for each 25 full-time faculty members or 500 full-time students

   _____   _____

   Comments:

   b. Approximately one clerical/technical staff member for each professional staff member

   _____   _____

   Comments:

   c. One part-time student assistant for each 150 students enrolled

   _____   _____

   Comments:

7. The director (principal professional) of the learning resources program should:
   a. Be a member of the college administrative team with appropriate rank and title

   _____   _____

Comments:

b. Report to the dean or vice-president having college-wide responsibility for academic leadership

_____ _____

Comments:

c. Develop the learning resources program annual budget

_____ _____

Comments:

d. Have a twelve-month contract

_____ _____

Comments:

8. The professional staff of the learning resources program should:
   a. Have rank, status, and benefits of other college employees

_____ _____

Comments:

b. Be assigned to learning resources program operations exclusively (i.e., not hold split assignments with
other administrative or instructional duties)

_____   _____

Comments:

c. Have assigned time for instructional development
assistance to the teaching faculty

_____   _____

Comments:

d. Serve on curriculum committees to provide liaison to
the learning resources program

_____   _____

Comments:

e. Be involved in the development and writing of proposals for off-campus funding

_____   _____

Comments:

f. Serve as catalyst in encouraging the teaching faculty
to use creative and varied instructional methods

_____   _____

Comments:

g. Have twelve-month contracts

_____   _____

Comments:

C. *Functions*   *Agree   Disagree*

9. The basic functions of the learning resources program
   include:
   a. Serving as a clearinghouse for all college-wide
   purchases of instructional materials and equipment

_____   _____

Comments:

b. Coordinating study skill centers or laboratories established to assist in student learning activities

_____   _____

Comments:

10. Some suggested policies of the learning resources program include:
a. Grouping materials by format and filing them on open shelves for easy patron access

_____   _____

Comments:

b. Making equipment necessary for proper use of materials accessible for use within the learning resources area and classrooms

_____   _____

Comments:

c. Opening the learning resources center during all class hours, evenings, weekends, holidays for use by students, faculty, and area residents who are not enrolled at the community college

Comments:

D. *Public Relations*   *Agree   Disagree*

11. The community college administration and personnel
should be informed of the learning resources center's:
a. Functions

                                                           _____   _____

Comments:

b. Services

          _____   _____

Comments:

c. Programs

          _____   _____

Comments:

d. Materials

          _____   _____

Comments:

e. Needs

_____   _____

Comments:

12. This communication should be accomplished by means of:
a. Annual report

_____   _____

Comments:

b. Statements of short and long-range goals

_____   _____

Comments:

c. Policy statements

_____   _____

Comments:

d. Faculty and student handbooks

Comments: _____ _____

e. Advisory committee

Comments: _____ _____

f. Reports and office meetings

Comments: _____ _____

g. Bibliographies

Comments: _____ _____

h. Displays

_____ _____

Comments:

i. Orientation sessions

_____ _____

Comments:

j. Inservice sessions

_____ _____

Comments:

13. The learning resources program should be a participating member of existing or future cooperatively established networks which will insure maximum accessibility and availability of instructional resources and services.

_____ _____

Comments:

E. *Instructional Development*

14. Instructional development should be encouraged by
providing the following:

_____   _____

Comments:

a. Establishment of teams of individuals possessing different competencies, experiences, and training for the
purpose of designing instructional programs.

_____   _____

Comments:

b. Allocation of a certain percentage of the college's
budget for instructional development activities

_____   _____

Comments:

c. Granting of release time from instructional teaching
assignments to faculty members engaged in major instructional development activities

_____   _____

Comments:

d. Provision of personal recognition to faculty and members of the learning resources program

_____   _____

Comments:

e. A portion of the teaching faculty evaluation form which relate to the use of media within a classroom setting

_____   _____

Comments:

f. Establishment on each college campus of a review process for initiating instructional change flexible enough to allow each person to design or redesign programs

_____   _____

Comments:

g. Provision that the teaching faculty have the freedom to develop their own course content and use methods befitting themselves which will meet the college's instructional goals and objectives

_____   _____

Comments:

h. Establishment of an inservice program which will assist in training staff in the process and procedures to be used in designing instructional innovation

_____   _____

Comments:

i. Develement of a process whereby locally produced/prepared instructional materials are evaluated

_____   _____

Comments:

15. Activities which are essential for achieving success in supporting or influencing instruction are:
a. Cooperation between learning resources center staff and the college faculty

_____   _____

Comments:

b. Offering a full range of services

_____   _____

Comments:

c. Designing, developing, and producing media

_____   _____

Comments:

d. Writing Proposals seeking outside funding for use in instructional development activities

_____   _____

Comments:

POSSIBLE ADDITIONAL CRITERIA

If you feel there are potential criteria not included within the five previously stated areas, please list them under the appropriate section below:

A. General:

B. Personnel:

C. Functions:
D. Public Relations
E. Instructional Development:

APPENDIX J.
Community College Profiles

A profile of each of the seven community colleges visited is provided to acquaint the reader with the location, population, objectives, and organization of the colleges and their learning resources programs.

Bergen Community College
Paramus, New Jersey
Sarah K. Thomson, Chairman, Library and
Learning Resources Department

The campus is located upon a 167-acre site on what formerly was the Orchard Hills Country Club. The new campus was officially opened for instruction on December 18, 1972. Located in a suburban environment adjacent to New York City, the college enrolls approximately 3,500 full-time and 4,500 part-time students.

In a September 1965 report to the State Board of Education made by the New Jersey State Commissioner of Education, it was stated that there was sufficient and reliable evidence of the need for a county college in Bergen County and that the county was financially able to construct and operate the proposed college. The college was projected to fulfill immediate and long-range educational needs of the citizens of the community.

The primary aims of Bergen Community College are to—

1. make two-year college education available to members of the community;
2. provide full- and part-time students with diversified programs of studies leading to a variety of educational and vocational goals;
3. offer programs of scholastic, vocational, personal, and community counseling;
4. use the resources of the institution to meet local needs;
5. supplement educational opportunities in the county and state.

Bergen Community College subscribes to the comprehensive community college concept which brings education beyond the high school level to all who can profit from it. It is also dedicated to the ideal that special services, such as continuing education programs, cultural activities, and counseling, should be made available to the entire community.

Bergen Community College realizes the need to develop and educate citizens prepared to meet the varied demands of a dynamic, technological age and to prepare young people and adults to undertake the obligations of intelligent citizenship and family life. The college offers diversified and useful educational experiences to meet its responsibilities to the individual and to society. High academic standards are maintained so that the student can transfer easily to the four-year college or be prepared for immediate and effective employment.

The college is aware of its total obligation to the student body and to the community at large. It serves as a cultural center dedicated to learning and service. Bergen Community College holds frequent lectures, symposia, musical and dramatic presentations, as well as exhibiting film festivals and workshops of general interest which encourage broad community participation. The college's proximity to centers of learning and areas rich in cultural activity enables it to draw fully on these resources while making its own contributions to them. Symbolic of this philosophy and purpose is the Library and Learning Resource Center which is located at the functional and geographical center of the campus. It is the intellectual nucleus around which the Colleg's educational programs revolve. The chairman for the Library and Learning Resource Center was the fourth person to be hired as the college began a year of development and organization prior to its first day of classes in September 1968.

The primary emphasis of the faculty is on effective instruction of students. Research and writing to reinforce instructional activities are important. Since the general welfare of the student is of paramount importance, emphasis on individual advisement and counseling is fundamental to the college's philosophy. Faculty members are selected not only for their academic qualifications and experience but also for their interest in maintaining close student-teacher relationships that will enable students to develop their full potential. To reach this goal, student counseling services are centralized under the Dean of Students.

Bergen Community College has been approved as an institution of higher learning by the New Jersey State Department of Higher Education and is fully accredited by the Middle States Association of Colleges and Secondary Schools.

City College of San Francisco
San Francisco, California
Mrs. Iole Matteucig, Assistant Dean of Library Services

The City College of San Francisco was established in 1935 and was founded to meet a sustained demand by the people of San Francisco to establish a public institution of higher learning that offered instruction on both the university and semi-professional levels.

Instruction began in August 1935 in temporary facilities at the University of California Extension Division Building at Galileo High School. Approximately 1,500 students were in attendance during the first semester. Escalating enrollment forced the use of other temporary facilities, and by 1939, classes were meeting in twenty-two locations. To overcome these difficult conditions, the San Francisco Board of Education approved a building program designed to meet the future needs of the college.

Acquisition of a fifty-six acre campus in Balboa Park, which is located south of the downtown area, marked the completion of the first step in this program. The first buildings had been planned for an enrollment of 2,500, but by 1940, approximately 3,200 students were in attendance. The national defense program and the subsequent entry of the United States into World War II led to a decline in enrollment, but by 1947, the influx of high school graduates and returning veterans swelled the student body beyond 5,500. To provide more classroom space, the college scheduled evening classes in a nearby school and acquired the United States Navy Waves Separation Center, which adjoined the campus.

Provision of funds by the San Francisco Unified School District, principally through school-bond elections and state and federal grants, enabled the college to continue its building program in order to accommodate enrollment which, in the spring of 1974, totaled approximately 14,000 students in the Day Division and approximately 6,500 students in the Evening Division.

City College of San Francisco is dedicated to the belief that higher education should make generally available whatever intellectual training people need and seek. It takes a responsibility as well for the general intellectual development of its graduates. Its curriculum is comprehensive and diverse.

The college offers two-year programs of study to meet the needs of its students and the city whose name it bears. In common with other schools of this kind, it offers the first two years of instruction leading to the bachelor's degree, while meeting educational needs not satisfied by universities, liberal arts colleges, or technical institutes. This special combination of services is reflected in the nature of the college, the diversity of its functions, the number and variety of its curricula, and its sensitivity to the educational requirements of those whom it serves. The college makes its opportunities available, tuition-free, to all resident high school graduates and to other mature resident persons prepared to undertake college work. Nonresidents of California, under the State Education Code, are required to pay tuition.

Within its resources, City College of San Francisco seeks to provide opportunities for each of its students to acquire and develop intellectual, ethical, social, and physical competencies so that they may live rich and useful lives. In offering these opportunities, the college intends—

1. to make the student aware of the disciplines that have occupied men's minds and to make him sufficiently familiar with at least one of them so that he will have both material and method for thought;
2. to assist the student in preparing for a career;
3. to bring forth in the student a facility in the languages of words and numbers so that he may communicate with his fellow men and develop an awareness of man's contribution to the world's cultures, past and present;
4. to assist the student in his physical development through the improvement of his physical skills and in increased health knowledge so that he may enjoy the benefits of physical and mental well-being to the fullest extent possible;
5. to provide the student with sufficient awareness and

understanding of American political principles and
their development for him to become a socially concerned and just citizen; and

6. to create an environment in which students of diverse
   backgrounds may attain the satisfaction of living to full
   capacity as individuals and as members of a broader
   community.

City College also intends to provide educational opportunities appropriate to the interests and needs of an ever-
changing community.

The program of studies offered by the City College of San
Francisco is accredited by the Western Association of
Schools and Colleges. In addition, semi-professional curricula are accredited, approved, or recognized by specialized agencies.

College of DuPage
Glen Ellyn, Illinois
Richard L. Ducote, Dean of Learning Resources

DuPage County lies directly west of Chicago. Great
changes in county growth and characteristics have taken
place in the recent years, and continued changes will have
an important bearing upon the educational needs of the
citizens. The district of the College of DuPage (DuPage
County and small portions of Will and Cook Counties) had
originally developed as primarily residential; however,
within the past few years industrial development has far
outpaced projections and now occupies a prominent place
within the area growth pattern. Many diversified small
industries, large manufacturers, numerous service industries, and several research centers have located within
DuPage County.

Following the passage of the Junior College Act in the Illinois General Assembly in 1965, the voters of ten high

school districts in DuPage County acted favorably on December 4, 1965, to create a junior college to serve the residents of the area. Soon several additional districts voted to be annexed into the district. These additions made the College of DuPage district one of the most populous districts in Illinois outside the city of Chicago, with its citizens numbering more than 700,000.

In September 1967, the college opened with an enrollment of 2,619 students. By 1974 the college's enrollment had grown to more than 12,000. In September 1969, after holding classes in rented facilities for two years, most of the college operation moved to interim campus buildings. Satellite teaching stations, including many district high schools for the continuing education program, are used as a method of bringing educational opportunities to all district residents.

During the summer of 1971, College of DuPage discarded the traditional organizational structure of discipline lines, (e.g., English Department, Humanities Department) and was reorganized into a cluster system by forming a series of small colleges, each of which provides a comprehensive educational program for its students. This plan supports the belief that the individual student's needs are met best through a more intimate and personalized atmosphere inherent in the small college cluster organization. There are seven cluster colleges. One, Alpha, is an experimental college enrolling about 200 students in nontraditional studies. Another, Extension, is organized to offer courses and programs in off-campus locations throughout the district. The other five are staffed to enroll about 1,200 full-time equivalent students each, making it possible for students and faculty to work closely together in achieving educational goals. This allows for greater personal attention to students by faculty. Each of the colleges offers a comprehensive program of curricular offerings including studies leading toward university transfer, career orientation, and general and continuing education.

After identifying his/her career interest, a student can expect to find one or another of the colleges with a complete program able to fulfill his need. Each college features areas of emphasis and offers related courses supporting such programs.

In addition to Alpha and Extension, the colleges and areas of career emphasis are:

Delta — Physical Science and Related Technologies, Humanities and Vocational

Kappa — Business

Omega — Media

Psi — Human Services

Sigma — Health

The college is accredited by the North Central Association of Colleges and Secondary Schools. College of DuPage is evaluated yearly by the Illinois Community College Board by submitting a detailed "Application for Recognition" and a "Report of Selected Data and Characteristics of Illinois Public Junior Colleges." In addition, the college receives a formal visit from members of the staff of the state board at least every fifth year.

A permanent campus is being developed on the college's 273-acre site. Construction of a seven-building complex is planned in phases, with the first phase having been completed in 1973.

College of DuPage is dedicated to the service of the community. Created by the community's need for the variety of educational programs that only a comprehensive junior college can supply, the college is committed to offer a full range of programs. The college will perform its functions best by providing each student with—

1. the maximum educational development of which he is capable;

2. the opportunity to examine critically the issues of a

dynamic society;

3. opportunities for leadership and participation in group decision-making;
4. recognition of individual and social rights and responsibilities;
5. an opportunity for experiences which increase his understanding of our cultural heritage;
6. an opportunity to acquire a useful vocational skill;
7. opportunities for vocational and leisure-time experiences; and
8. guidance in the formulation of personal career goals.

The college must be responsible not only to the needs of the students but also to the needs of the community. Hence, it will seek to stimulate the intellectual and cultural life of the community, attempt to meet the employment needs of local businesses and institutions, and invite local participation in the formulation of its programs.

College of DuPage is committed to—

1. guaranteeing to every individual equality of opportunity through education experiences adjusted to his level of readiness; and
2. assisting in the satisfaction of human needs and in the resolution of societal problems which exist and/or evolve.

As a student-centered and future-oriented institution of higher learning, the college is—

accessible to an ever-increasing proportion of community members.

comprehensive in terms of the provisions established to meet the changing individual and community needs and the objectives of the institution. In everything that it seeks to do, the college must strive to be open, receptive, participative, and flexible.

community-centered in its service concepts and orientation, in its control and support, in its interests, and in its approaches to evolving service opportunities.

committed to supplementing societal efforts to promote life-long learning and change on the part of community members.

The college provides the following services: general education programs suitable to a wide variety of students; university-parallel course offerings; specific career programs; developmental programs to assist students in achieving academic proficiencies; advising and counseling; and public service programs.

The College of DuPage believes it is essential that the college:
- functions as an integral part of the community;
- involves the community in the fulfillment of its mission;
- establishes goals and objectives that focus on future horizons, changing conditions, and evolving needs;
- justifies proposals for change and requests for resources in terms of community values, interests, and needs.

Greenfield Community College
Greenfield, Massachusetts
Margaret E. C. Howland, Chairman, Division of Learning Resources

Greenfield Community College is located in a rural setting in the beautiful and historic Pioneer Valley of western Massachusetts. It is one of fifteen community colleges operating under the authority of the Massachusetts Board of Regional Community Colleges and supported by the Commonwealth of Massachusetts.

Opening in September 1962 with 125 students, the college, which is located on an eighty-acre site, now has a current enrollment of 1,400 full-time and 361 part-time students. Greenfield Community College moved into its $16.5 million permanent facility in August 1974. The building is terraced up a hillside and has five levels in the core area which houses executive offices, the college library, computer center, audiovisual center, TV center, college store, and cafeteria. The north and south academic wings contain six faculty-student modules which serve as gathering places and focal points for college activities. Exterior multilevel courtyards provide a relaxing surrounding.

The present construction was built to accommodate from 1,500 to 2,000 students. Plans for future construction include physical education facilities and an auditorium.

The college offers a comprehensive program of studies and related supporting services. The services of the college are available to students of varying ages, both full-time and part-time. The instructors make use of many strategies, recognizing that students learn in various ways.

The college is dedicated to offering quality education at the lowest possible cost to students in the region and from other sections of the commonwealth. Enrollment is open to out-of-state students.

Greenfield Community College is accredited by the New England Association of Schools and Colleges. It is served by an advisory board of regional residents appointed by the governor.

Greenfield Community College believes in people—in their dignity, individuality and diversity, in their freedom to think and to explore, in their need for knowledge and continuing growth, and in their responsibility to contribute positively to society. The college motto expresses the essence of that philosophy: "The right to think—the will to learn."

The community college's mission includes the provision of programs for students desiring transfer to the upper division of a baccalaureate degree program, and programs designed to prepare students for a variety of career positions in which an associate degree is necessary or desirable. To this end, there are currently sixteen associate degree programs being offered. The instructional program is organized around six divisions—one being learning resources.

Florissant Valley Community College
St. Louis, Missouri
Betty Duvall, Associate Dean,
Instructional Resources

The fourteen-year history of Florissant Valley Community College as a member of the Junior College District of St. Louis is characterized by rapid growth, educational innovation, and a tradition of community services.

Committed to the idea of a comprehensive community college system, determined citizens participated in efforts to bring about the creation of institutions to meet post-secondary educational needs of the community. Enabling legislation was enacted by the Missouri Legislature, and in 1962, the Junior College District was approved by district voters.

Three colleges resulted—Florissant in suburban north county, Forest Park in the city of St. Louis, and Meramec in the southwest part of the county. Since 1962, each college has greatly expanded its operations, beginning with rented buildings, moving to temporary campus structures, and finally to modern, well equipped permanent facilities.

Florissant Valley Community college opened in February 1963 and offered only evening courses. More than 250 students enrolled in those first classes taught at an area high school. The enrollment grew to 750 the following semester.

February 1975 found the enrollment of full-time students just over 3,000 and part-time students at nearly 5,200.

A permanent campus location was purchased in 1963, and construction of temporary buildings began. During the next four years, the temporary structures, with several additional trailers, served the college as classrooms, offices, and student centers.

In 1965, district voters approved a $47.2 million bond issue (at that time the largest bond issue of its type ever passed) to construct permanent structures on the three campuses. Construction at Florissant Valley began in April 1966, and the first three buildings were in use in 1967–68. The gradual shift from temporary buildings to permanent structures continued throughout the next three years.

Each of the three colleges within the district is headed by a vice-president who reports to a district-wide president. Overall district policies and procedures are established through a management-by-objectives program.

As a comprehensive community college district, the Junior College District of St. Louis is concerned with the post–high school educational needs of the community it serves. The district accepts its responsibility for leadership and purposes to develop and maintain a collegiate program sufficiently flexible to adjust to the changing educational needs of the area. To fulfill these needs, the district offers academic, technical-vocational, and cultural courses, all directed toward the betterment of the student, and thus of the community.

Florissant Valley is dedicated to quality instruction and, therefore, to the continuing improvement of instruction and of the functions that facilitate teaching and learning. It promotes instructional and institutional research as a means of improving its ongoing functions. To assist in reaching its instructional goals, Florissant Valley Community College has established the following:

1. *College Level Curricula*-offers courses and curricula at the college level only, except for certain developmental work intended to prepare high school graduates (or the equivalent) for college-level curricula
2. *Two-Year Programs*-offers courses normally taught in the lower division (first and second year) of senior colleges and universities, together with occupational curricula that can normally be completed within two calendar years of college level work
3. *Serving the Community*-is responsive to the educational, cultural, civic, recreational, and other needs of the immediate community
4. *Open to All*-accepts any resident of the district who is a high school graduate (or the equivalent) regardless of high school record or placement test score. (However, the college reserves the right to guide the placement of students into courses and curricula that seem appropriate considering specific preparation.)
5. *Comprehensive Offerings*-attempts to meet the needs of students with a wide range of abilities, interests, and goals through its college and university parallel curricula, its occupational programs, its developmental program, its continuing education offerings, and student services.

Florissant Valley Community College is fully accredited by the North Central Association of Colleges and Secondary Schools.

Lane Community College
Eugene, Oregon
Del Matheson, Head Librarian Learning Resource Center

Lane Community College was established in 1964 as a public, two-year coeducational institution. The district encompasses a 5,000–square mile area which includes Lane County, stretching from the Pacific Ocean to the Cascade Mountains. The college serves a population of about 237,000 persons. The college's enrollment is approximately 6,100 full-time students.

As one of Oregon's thirteen publicly supported community colleges, Lane operates under the general direction of the Oregon Board of Education. The state board handles requests for legislative appropriations, establishes standards for distribution of that support, and creates and implements guidelines for instructor and course approval.

On its 282-acre suburban Eugene campus, the college has 655,000 square feet under one roof. The modern $25 million campus was dedicated in 1969. It has been cited for its ease of access for the handicapped and for its landscaping. Construction monies were generated from local taxes and state and federal grants. Outreach centers are maintained in three locations and a skills center is located in one community.

The college offers a comprehensive curriculum which includes more than forty technical-vocational and sixty college transfer programs. The college is truly a part of its community. Its students range in age from the teens to the retirement years, and they use the college throughout life for initial training, refresher courses, and retraining; for avocational, recreational, and cultural pursuits; and for community betterment activities.

The college places educational opportunities within the financial, geographic, academic, and psychological reach of its community. Its tuition is low; its teaching locations are within close commuting distance; its remedial facilities and student-centered faculty reflect concern and interest for each student.

Lane Community College provides a wide range of career education and training suitable to varying levels of competency in preparation for employment in technical and vocational fields. Lane offers lower-division college transfer courses which parallel the requirements of the State System of Higher Education. General courses, community services and programs, and extra-curricular activities are offered for those who desire to broaden their educational and cultural experiences or to continue life-long learning.

Lane Community College provides developmental and remedial education which affords opportunities for entry into other areas. Lane offers continuing education courses to provide for job improvement, apprentice-related instruction, occupational extension, and personal growth. Counseling services to assist students and residents of the community in self-evaluation and attainment of their personal and educational goals are provided. Numerous cultural activities are offered to the residents of the college region.

Lane Community College's growing national reputation has earned it membership in the League for Innovation in the Community College. As a member of the League, Lane Community College participates with America's best community colleges in the exchange of innovative ideas and practices. The college is accredited by the Northwest Association of Secondary and Higher Schools.

Lane serves more than twenty thousand individuals each year in credit and adult education classes. The 1973–74 enrollment for credit programs was 10,317; for adult education, 11,398. Unduplicated head count, estimated, for the college's first nine years—1965–1974—was 99,545. That included 48,541 in credit programs and 51,004 in adult education.

The typical credit student is a Lane County resident. Caucasian, freshman, male, single, age 25, who attends school full-time. That profile emerges from an analysis of the 6,750 individuals who enrolled in the fall term 1974 for one or more credit courses. The students were 58 percent male, and 64 percent of the total were attending full-time. A larger share of the men, 68 percent compared to 58 percent for women, were attending full-time.

Prince George's Community College
Largo, Maryland
Leah K. Nekritz, Director, Learning Resources

Largo, now rural in character, is being affected by rapid suburban growth. Once relying upon small town commerce and an agriculture system based upon tobacco and truck farming, the area has rapidly broadened its economic base to include research and government service industries. The area's close proximity to the District of Columbia has stimulated growth. With a growing population, now numbering more than 750,000, Prince George's County claims a proud historical background and looks forward to meeting the challenges of the future in all areas of social, cultural, and business activities.

Prince George's Community College started in a high school building in 1958 with only evening course offerings which were almost exclusively in the college transfer program area. Prince George's Community College began operation with an initial enrollment of 185 students, 12 faculty members, a dean, and a director of student personnel. The first associate of arts degrees were given in June of 1960, by which time both faculty and student body had doubled in size. In 1964, plans for a permanent campus at Largo were approved. It was not until 1967, when Prince George's moved onto its permanent campus, that career programs were developed. Today the college enrolls almost ten thousand students at its 150-acre site.

Programs of study are organized around two options: (1) liberal arts and science (transfer) and (2) technical and career education (career). The college provides extensive assistance to students in planning a program of study. Prince George's Community College is dedicated to the provision of an environment where learning opportunities are available to all members of the community who wish to take part. The college provides additional workshops, seminars, and conferences through its community services area.

Prince George's Community College operates under the following guidelines:

A. Philosophy
   1. Creation of a total educational environment and commitment in helping each student realize his maximum potential.
   2. Assuming leadership in responding to community needs in the face of a changing society.

B. Objectives
   1. Implementation of effective learning programs by awareness of new developments in curricula, teaching methods, and teaching tools.
   2. Maintenance of close student/faculty relationships.
   3. Encouragement of individual thought and action in each student.
   4. Enlargement of the student's understanding of mankind's history and experience, and development of a student's perspective of himself and his relation to society.

C. Programs
   1. Academic transfer programs to four-year colleges and universities.
   2. Technical, vocational, and paraprofessional programs culminating with an associate of arts degree.
   3. Extracurricular activities for enlargement of the student's interests.
   4. Activities for adults who desire personal enrichment along with a continuing education.

5. Service programs responding to community problems and needs.

The college was accredited by the Maryland State Department of Education in 1972 and by the Middle States Association of Colleges and Secondary Schools.

List of Works Cited

1. Allen, Kenneth W. *Use of Community College Libraries*. Hamden, Connecticut: Linnet Books, 1971.
2. The American College Testing Program, Inc. *The Two-Year College and Its Students: An Empirical Report*. Monograph Two. Iowa City: 1969.
3. The Carnegie Commission on Higher Education. *The Open Door College*. New York: McGraw-Hill, 1970.
4. Cohen, Arthur M. *Dateline '79: Heretical Concepts for the Community College*. Beverly Hills: Glencoe Press, 1969.
5. Crouch, Howard Hayes. "Criteria for the Construction of Community Junior College Curricula." Ed.D. dissertation, The Ohio State University, 1964.
6. Ducote, Richard. *Promoting Media Utilization*. Boone, North Carolina: Appalachian University, 1970.
7. Evans, N. Dean, and Neagley, Ross L. *Planning and Developing Innovative Community Colleges*. Englewood Cliffs, New Jersey: Prentice-Hall, 1973.
8. Fretwell, Elbert K., Jr. *Founding Public Junior Colleges*. Teachers College, Columbia University: Bureau of Publications, 1954.
9. Fusaro, Janice F. "Toward Library-College Media Centers; Proposal for the Nation's Community Colleges." *Junior College Journal*, April 1970, pp. 40–44.
10. Gleazer, Edmund J., Jr. *This is the Community col-*

lege. Boston: Houghton Mifflin, 1968.

11. Gorena, Ame and Rosemary Root. *Prescriptive Inservice Handbook* (Final Report USOE Grant No G 007702302). Oklahoma City: State Department of Education, 1978.

12. Hale, Charles E. "A Survey: Kentucky's Junior/Community College Libraries." *Kentucky Library Association Bulletin*, October 1970, pp. 13–21.

13. Harlacher, Ervin L. *The Community Dimension of the Community College*. Englewood Cliffs, New Jersey: Prentice-Hall, 1969.

14. Havelock, Ronald G. *The Change Agent's Guide to Innovation in Education*. Englewood Cliffs, New Jersey: Educational Technology Publications, 1973, p. 279.

15. Henry, Nelson B. (ed.). *The Public Junior College— The Fifty-fifth Yearbook of the National Society for the Study of Education*. Chicago: the National Society for the Study of Education, 1956.

16. Horn, Andrew H., *et al. Report of a Brief Survey of the El Camino College Library*. El Camino College, California: University of California Clearinghouse for Junior College Information, 1966.

17. Illinois Library Association. *A Multi-media Survey of the Community College Libraries of the State of Illinois*. Chicago: Prairie State College, 1970.

18. Joyce, Bruce, and Weil, Marsha. *Models of Teaching*. Englewood Cliffs, New Jersey: Prentice-Hall, 1972.

19. Kelley, Win and Wilbur, Leslie. *Teaching in the Community-Junior College*. New York: Appleton-Century-Crofts, 1970.

20. Kellogg, Virgil. *Educational Media Programs at Iowa's Area Community Colleges and Vocational Schools, 1971–72*. Des Moines: Department of Public Instruction, 1972, p. 42.

21. Keuscher, Robert Edward. "An Appraisal of Some Dimensions of Systems Theory as Indicators of the

Tendency to Innovate in Selected Public Junior colleges." Ed.D. dissertation, University of California, 1968.

22. Lane Community College. *Procedures for Community College Planning & Curriculum Development.* Washington, D.C.: Bureau of Occupational & Adult Education (DHEW/OE), 1977.

23. Lyle, Guy R. *The Administration of the College Library.* New York: H.W. Wilson, 1961.

24. Miles, Matthew B. (ed.). *Innovation in Education.* New York: Columbia University, 1964.

25. Monroe, Charles R. *Profile of the Community College.* San Francisco: Jossey-Bass, 1972.

26. National Council for Staff, Program & Organizational Development. *Annual Report.* Florida Junior College at Jacksonville, 1977–78.

27. O'Baniom, Terry. *Organizing Staff Development Programs that Work.* Washington, D.C.: American Association of Community & Junior Colleges, 1978.

28. Raines, Max R. *Survey of Leading Library and Learning Resource Centers in Forty Community Colleges.* Higher Education, Michigan State University. East Lansing: Max R. Raines, 1972, p. 21.

29. Reeves, Pamela. "Junior Colleges, Libraries Enter the Seventies." *College and Research Libraries,* 34 (1973): 7–15.

30. Wheeler, Helen Rippier. *The Community College Library: A Plan for Action.* Hamden, Connecticut: The Shoe String Press, 1965.

31. Wheeler, Helen Rippier. "The Community College Library; An Appraisal of Current Practice." Ed. D. dissertation, Teacher's College, Columbia University, 1964.

32. Zwerling, L. Steven. *Second Best.* New York: McGraw/Hill, 1976.

Index

DATE DUE